Discovering
FRENCH
with

HARRAP

PLANNED AND PRODUCED BY
BOOKMAKER

EDITORIAL DIRECTION
Marie Garagnoux • Patrick Michel-Dansac
WITH
Françoise Avril

COMPILED BY
Bookmaker

TRANSLATION
Maggie Doyle

COLOURS BY
Jean-Pierre Sachse

LAYOUT
Design:
Claudine Roy
Produced by:
Michèle Andrault • Monique Michel-Dansac

OTHERS CONTRIBUTORS
Sylvie Decaux • Dominique Bluher • Elida Mannevy • Brian Mott •
Béatrice Leroy • Christine Ehm • Régine Ferrandis •
Mathilde Kemula • Bernard Wooding • Catherine Chevalot

PRODUCTION
Véronique Celton

TYPESETTING AND COLOUR SEPARATION
Charente Photogravure

© THE WALT DISNEY COMPANY, 1991
First published by
HARRAP BOOKS Ltd, Chelsea House,
26 Market Square, Bromley, Kent BR1 1NA

ISBN 0 245-60379-4

Note to the reader

Mickey, Donald and all their pals are about to help you discover the French language.

You can follow their adventures in the cartoon strips found throughout this book which will introduce you to spoken French. On each page, one of the cartoons has been enlarged and changed (you can have fun spotting the differences) ; the key words to remember are grouped around the big picture.

Before setting off in your friends' footsteps, read the instructions on page 5 carefully. The guide on page 4 is intended in particular for your parents and teachers.

Foreword

*D*iscovering *French with Walt Disney* is a vocabulary book for 8 to 13-year-olds, whether beginners or more advanced learners. It includes 1000 words from all grammatical categories (nouns, verbs, adjectives, adverbs, etc.) which have been selected by a team of language teaching specialists. The words, and the sentences in which they appear, correspond to the recommended contents of school curricula. The selection also takes into account the interests and everyday life of children in the 8 to 13 age group.

Each page of the book has been designed to further the joint goals of teaching a basic vocabulary and introducing common expressions : there is a large drawing illustrating the words to be learnt, and a comic strip showing idiomatic phrases in the speech bubbles.

This work is a practical tool which offers the young reader a set of useful guidelines :

• Organisation by areas of meaning puts each new word into a specific context, at once linguistic and visual, revealing its meaning in relation to associated words.

• In the vocabulary pages, the reader discovers original illustrations from the Walt Disney Studios including his or her favourite characters. The authors paid special attention to the quality of the artwork, legibility and careful selection of information.

• Essential basic information such as conjugations, numbers, days and months, etc., are given in separate appendices.

• Two bilingual indexes at the back of the book make up a complete dictionary of its words, and pronunciation is given using international phonetic transcription.

The Walt Disney characters bring their own humour and appeal to this book, which is intended to be, above all, a way to learn French vocabulary and have fun at the same time.

How to use this book

This vocabulary book includes 1000 words, broken down into 10 chapters, each with its own special theme. To learn words about a specific subject, just turn to the relevant chapter about that theme. The chapters go from pages 7 to 93 :

The subjects in each chapter are listed on the first page of the chapter. For example, this is the list of subjects on page 7, which is the first page of the chapter on "the house" : the garden, the house, in the house, the sitting room, the bedroom, in bed, the kitchen, the bathroom.
These subjects are illllustrated by a large picture surrounded by French words and sentences and their translations.

French word

translation of the word

French sentence

translation of the sentence

Under the illustration, a comic strip presents dialogues : the French text comes in the speech bubbles, the translation below.

French dialogue in speech bubbles

translation of the dialogue

All the vocabulary words are given in alphabetical order in the two indexes (on pages 101 to 111), along with their translation. If you need the exact translation of a word, simply use the indexes as if you were looking the words up in a dictionary.
You will also find the conjugation tables, the lists of numbers, days and months, as well as phonetics symbols on pages 95 to 99.

la maison • the house

le jardin • the garden

Il plante un arbre.
He is planting a tree.

le râteau
rake

l'arrosoir
watering can

la pelle
shovel

la haie
hedge

la pelouse
lawn

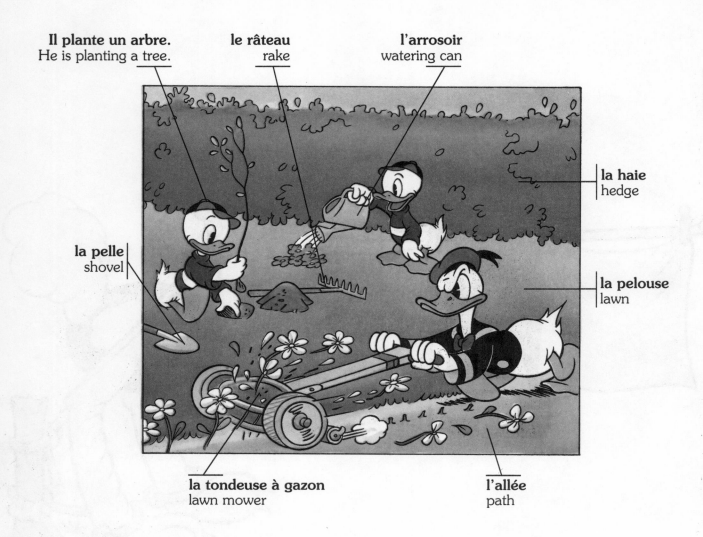

la tondeuse à gazon
lawn mower

l'allée
path

Riri arrose les fleurs.
Huey is watering the flowers.

C'est le printemps, ils sont dans le jardin.
It is springtime; they are in the garden.

– 'Bye Donald! See you soon!
– 'Bye Daisy!

– Donald

– She loves me… She loves me not…
She loves me…
– She loves me not!

la maison • the house

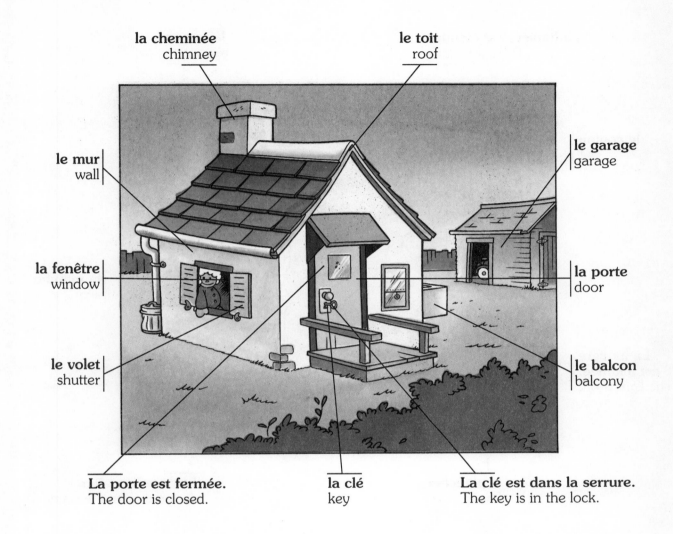

la cheminée
chimney

le toit
roof

le mur
wall

le garage
garage

la fenêtre
window

la porte
door

le volet
shutter

le balcon
balcony

La porte est fermée.
The door is closed.

la clé
key

La clé est dans la serrure.
The key is in the lock.

Donald ne peut pas habiter dans cette maison.
Donald cannot live in this house.

– What a lovely house!
– For rent

– You want to rent a house? I can sell you one for only $150.
– Impossible! You can't buy a house for that price!

– You don't believe me? Here's the deed!

– I'll take it!

– Doll's house
– For rent

dans la maison • in the house

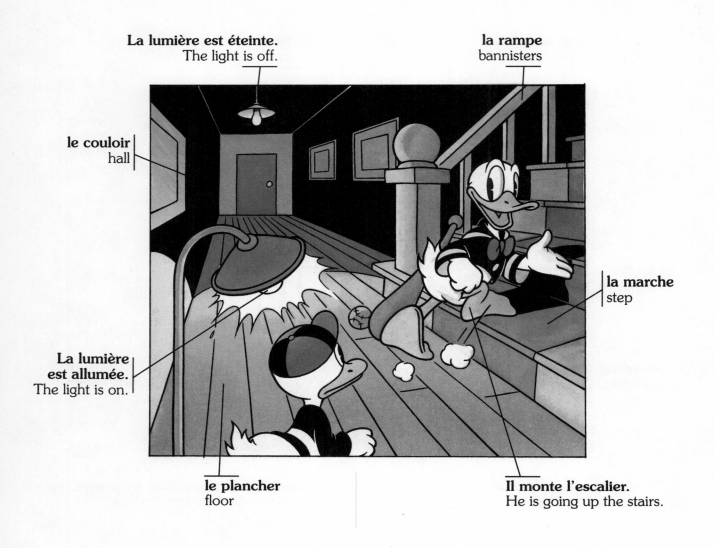

La lumière est éteinte.
The light is off.

la rampe
bannisters

le couloir
hall

la marche
step

La lumière est allumée.
The light is on.

le plancher
floor

Il monte l'escalier.
He is going up the stairs.

Le couloir est étroit et sombre.
The hall is narrow and dark.

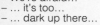

– We're afraid…
– … it's too…
– … dark up there…

– Don't be frightened! Watch me!

la salle de séjour • the sitting-room

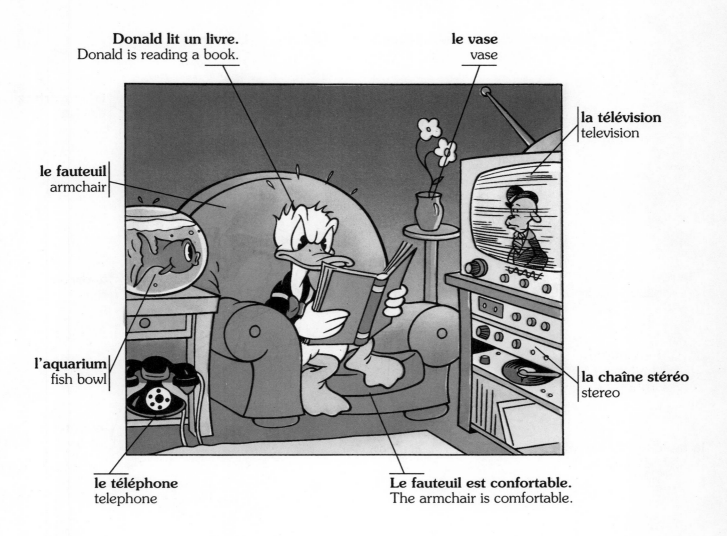

Donald lit un livre.
Donald is reading a book.

le vase
vase

la télévision
television

le fauteuil
armchair

l'aquarium
fish bowl

la chaîne stéréo
stereo

le téléphone
telephone

Le fauteuil est confortable.
The armchair is comfortable.

Donald est assis.
Donald is sitting down.

Le poisson rouge regarde la télévision !
The goldfish is watching television!

– That fish is driving me mad!

– Stop staring at me!

la chambre • the bedroom

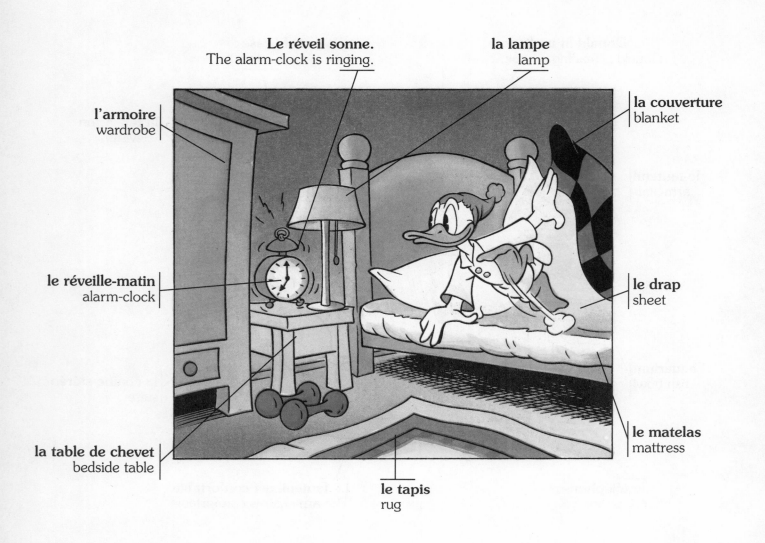

Le réveil sonne.
The alarm-clock is ringing.

la lampe
lamp

l'armoire
wardrobe

la couverture
blanket

le réveille-matin
alarm-clock

le drap
sheet

la table de chevet
bedside table

le matelas
mattress

le tapis
rug

Donald se lève.
Donald is getting up.

Il va bientôt se recoucher.
He will go back to bed soon.

– It's time!

– A little exercise…

– … to wake me up…

– Uh!

au lit • in bed

Donald est fatigué, il bâille.
Donald is tired; he is yawning.

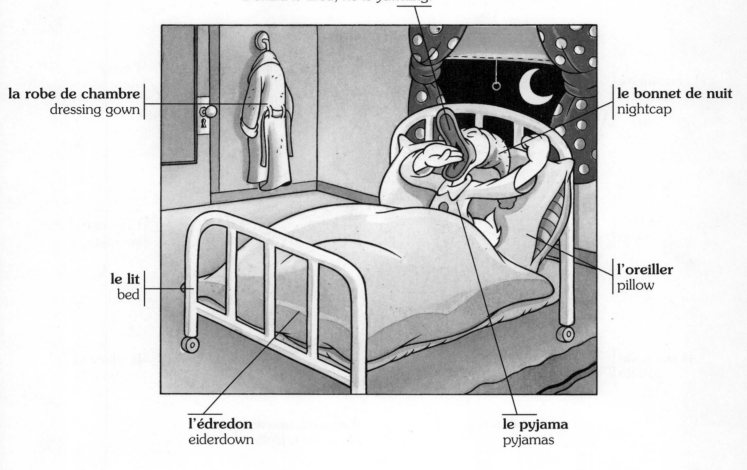

la robe de chambre
dressing gown

le bonnet de nuit
nightcap

le lit
bed

l'oreiller
pillow

l'édredon
eiderdown

le pyjama
pyjamas

Il est tard, c'est la nuit.
It is late; it is nighttime.

Il va dormir.
He is going to sleep.

– Get out of here, you horrible beast!
Let me get some sleep!

la cuisine • the kitchen

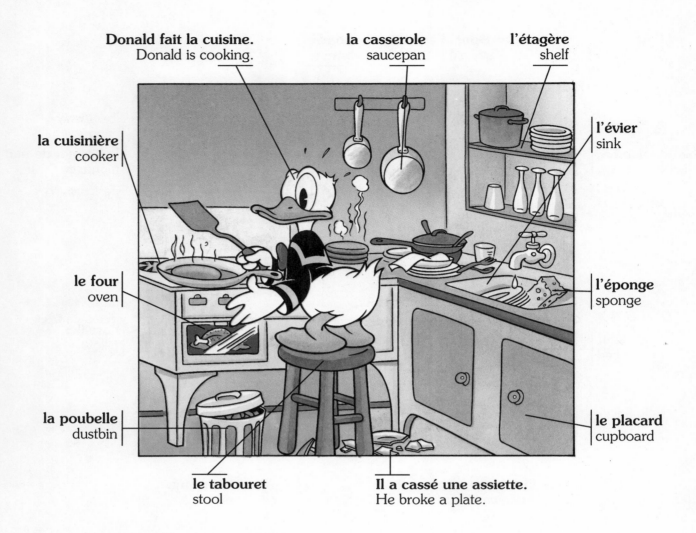

Donald fait la cuisine.
Donald is cooking.

la casserole
saucepan

l'étagère
shelf

la cuisinière
cooker

l'évier
sink

le four
oven

l'éponge
sponge

la poubelle
dustbin

le placard
cupboard

le tabouret
stool

Il a cassé une assiette.
He broke a plate.

Les verres sont rangés sur l'étagère.
The glasses are kept on the shelf.

La vaisselle n'est pas faite.
The dishes are not done.

– It's time…
– … to take our…
– … medicine, Uncle Donald.

– What a pleasant surprise… no one is making a face!
– Yum!

– 'Bye!
– 'Bye! This cake will taste better with some cream…

– Ugh!… Ah!

la salle de bains • the bathroom

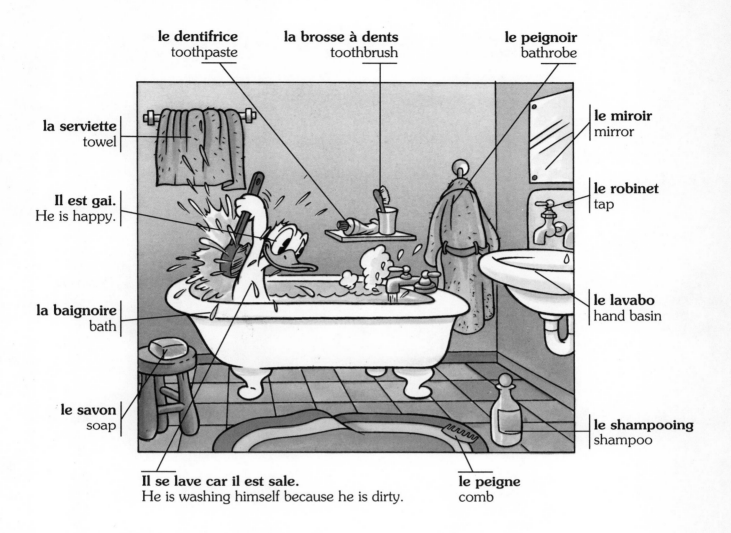

le dentifrice
toothpaste

la brosse à dents
toothbrush

le peignoir
bathrobe

la serviette
towel

le miroir
mirror

Il est gai.
He is happy.

le robinet
tap

la baignoire
bath

le lavabo
hand basin

le savon
soap

le shampooing
shampoo

Il se lave car il est sale.
He is washing himself because he is dirty.

le peigne
comb

Donald est propre ; il prend un bain.
Donald is clean; he is having a bath.

Il se brosse les dents deux fois par jour.
He brushes his teeth twice a day.

– ZZZZ!

– ZZZZ!

la ville • the town

la rue • the street

l'immeuble
building

le feu de signalisation
traffic light

le trottoir
pavement

la voiture
car

l'agent de police
policeman

le carrefour
crossroads

Donald demande son chemin à l'agent de police.
Donald is asking the policeman for directions.

Il lui montre le chemin.
He is showing him the way.

Il n'y a pas d'embouteillage !
There is no traffic jam!

Il est interdit de traverser quand le feu est vert.
It is forbidden to cross when the light is green.

– No parking

– Car Park

– Post office
– Postmen's bicycles only

la circulation • traffic

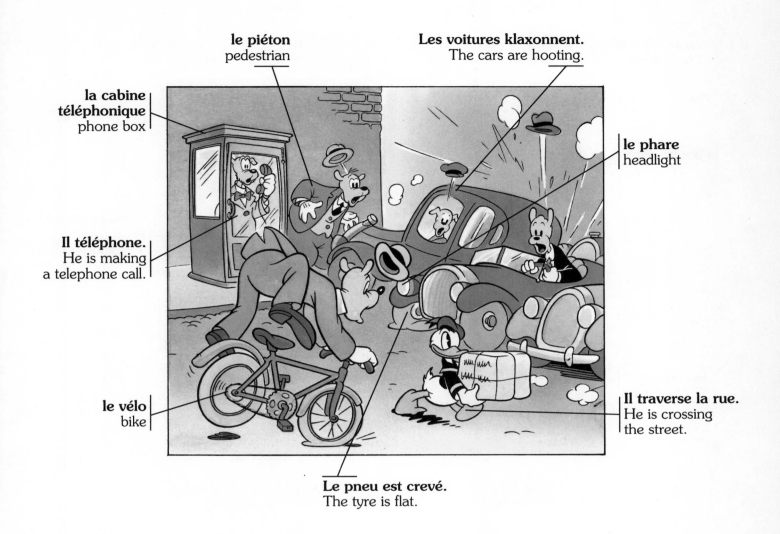

le piéton
pedestrian

Les voitures klaxonnent.
The cars are hooting.

la cabine téléphonique
phone box

le phare
headlight

Il téléphone.
He is making a telephone call.

le vélo
bike

Il traverse la rue.
He is crossing the street.

Le pneu est crevé.
The tyre is flat.

Donald a provoqué un embouteillage.
Donald has caused a traffic jam.

Il fait croire que son paquet contient de la dynamite.
He gets them to think there is dynamite in the parcel.

– There's only
one way out...

– Danger Dynamite

les magasins • shops

Il y a une seule boulangerie dans cette rue.
There is only one bakery on this street.

la boucherie
butcher's shop

l'épicerie
grocer's shop

la boulangerie
bakery

Cette boutique est fermée.
This shop is closed.

le boulanger
baker

le boucher
butcher

Donald fait les courses.
Donald is shopping.

Il y a de nombreux magasins dans cette rue.
There are a lot of shops in this street.

Donald n'aime pas aller au supermarché.
Donald does not like going to the supermarket.

– This chicken weighs two kilos.
– I'm going to check!
– Stuffed chicken

– Butcher's
– Opening hours

– Don't be offended! I just wanted to be sure.

– If you didn't shoot it…
– … why is there buckshot…
– … in the stuffing?

l'argent • money

Il vend un timbre à Donald.
He is selling Donald a stamp.

le vendeur
salesperson

le billet
bank note

le comptoir
counter

la caissière
cashier

le portefeuille
wallet

la pièce
coin

Elle paie la caissière.
She is paying the cashier.

le porte-monnaie
purse

la caisse
cash register

Donald achète un timbre.
Donald is buying a stamp.

Le lait est cher, le sucre est bon marché.
The milk is expensive, the sugar is cheap.

– May I have a two cent stamp?

– Your change!

à la gare • at the station

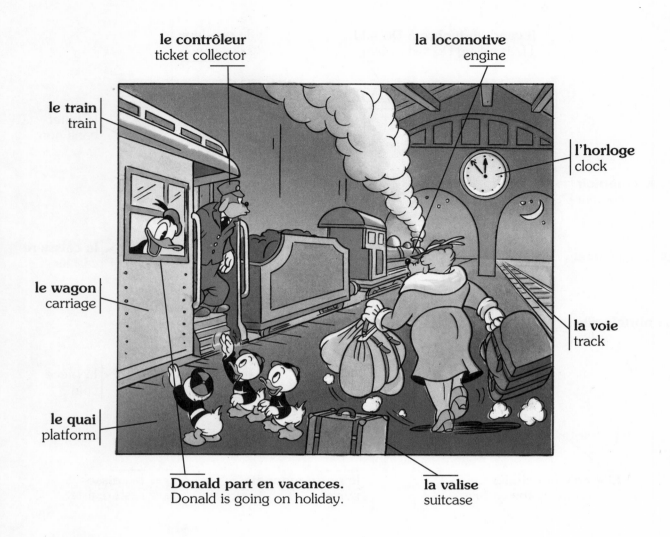

le contrôleur
ticket collector

la locomotive
engine

le train
train

l'horloge
clock

le wagon
carriage

la voie
track

le quai
platform

Donald part en vacances.
Donald is going on holiday.

la valise
suitcase

La dame se dépêche, elle est en retard.
The woman is in a hurry; she is late.

Ses bagages sont lourds.
Her luggage is heavy.

– See you soon!
– 'Bye…
– Uncle…
– Donald!

– I've forgotten
my suitcase!

– Quick! The train
is leaving!

les moyens de transport • transport

Il conduit l'autobus.
He is driving the bus.

le panneau
road sign

le taxi
taxi

le passager
passenger

la moto
motorcycle

le conducteur
driver

l'autobus
bus

le camion
lorry

le passage pour piétons
zebra crossing

Ils attendent l'autobus.
They are waiting for the bus.

Le panneau indique les directions.
The road sign gives the directions.

La petite fille est entre le monsieur et la dame.
The little girl is between the gentleman and the lady.

– Bus stop

– Bus stop

– Bus stop

23

l'école • the school

la salle de classe • the classroom

C'est le meilleur élève de la classe.
He is top of the class.

Elle efface le tableau.
She is cleaning the blackboard.

le tableau
blackboard

l'élève
pupil

la maîtresse
schoolteacher

Elle tourne la page.
She is turning
the page.

le bureau
desk

la page
page

l'élève
pupil

Il écrit.
He is writing.

Les élèves sont dans la salle de classe.
The pupils are in the classroom.

Les élèves travaillent bien.
The pupils are working hard.

– I'm going to see the headmaster and find out
how Li'l Davy's doing at school…

– Thank you for your help… school is an
excellent influence on Li'l Davy!
– Well…

– I don't know if school has influenced Li'l Davy, but Li'l
Davy has influenced the school!

la récréation · playtime

Le professeur surveille la cour.
The teacher is watching the playground.

Il court.
He is running.

**Les enfants
font la ronde.**
The children are
dancing in a ring.

Il joue aux billes.
He is playing marbles.

Michou a posé ses livres par terre.
Morty has put his books on the ground.

C'est un ami de Michou.
He is Morty's friend.

C'est l'heure de la récréation.
It is playtime.

Les enfants s'amusent.
The children are having fun.

– So… You're the new kid?

– That's right! Any more questions?

– What did you learn at school today, Morty?
– That you can't go by appearances!

le calcul • arithmetic

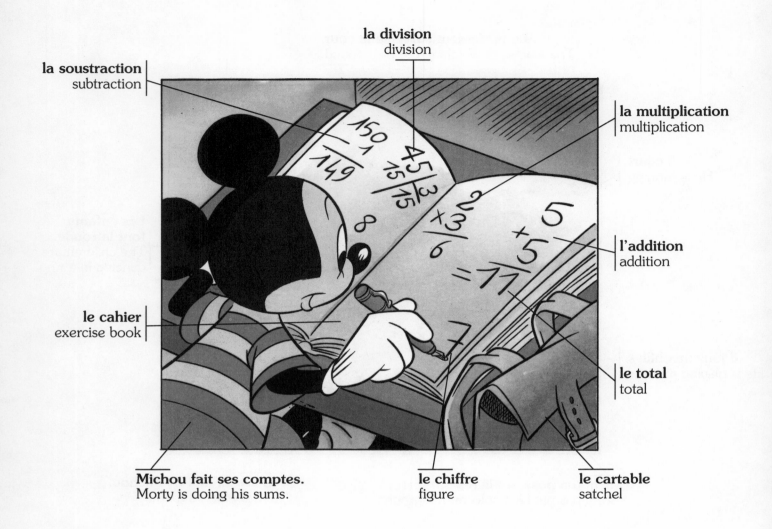

la division
division

la soustraction
subtraction

la multiplication
multiplication

l'addition
addition

le cahier
exercise book

le total
total

Michou fait ses comptes.
Morty is doing his sums.

le chiffre
figure

le cartable
satchel

Il a fait une erreur dans une opération.
He has made a mistake in one sum.

– Do you want me to help you with your homework?
– X has three dollars pocket money per week.

– Bus fare, pens, sweets, a film a week…
X can't do it!
– That's what I thought!

– Thanks for the raise, Mickey!

les couleurs • colours

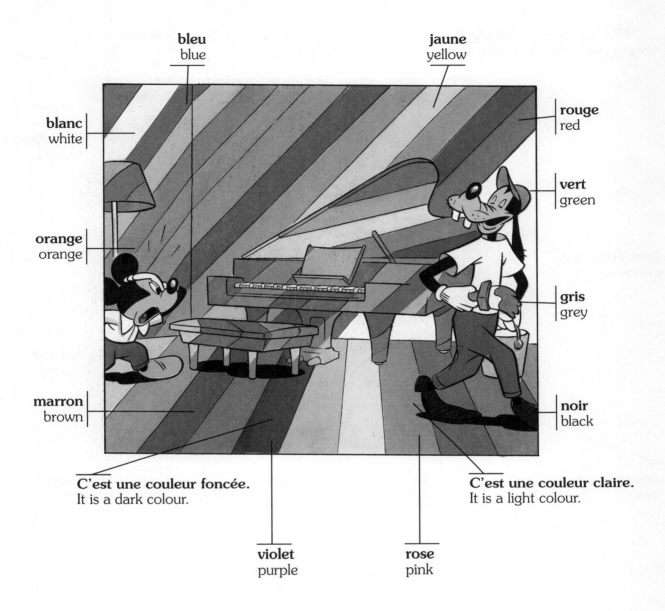

bleu
blue

jaune
yellow

blanc
white

rouge
red

vert
green

orange
orange

gris
grey

marron
brown

noir
black

C'est une couleur foncée.
It is a dark colour.

C'est une couleur claire.
It is a light colour.

violet
purple

rose
pink

– Good luck! I hope you'll do a good job!
– What do you mean by that? I paint the best stripes in town!

– Later…
– I don't know why, but I always worry when he does a job for me…

– You said you wanted a good job done… Well, here it is!

les formes • shapes

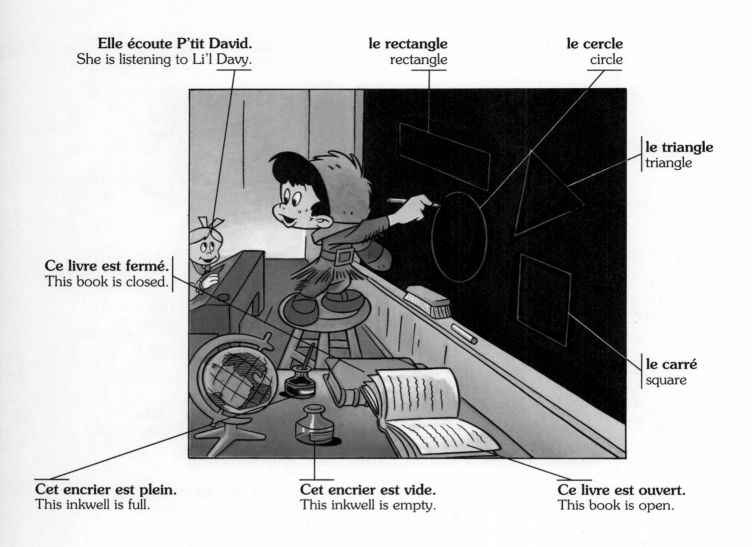

Elle écoute P'tit David.
She is listening to Li'l Davy.

le rectangle
rectangle

le cercle
circle

le triangle
triangle

Ce livre est fermé.
This book is closed.

le carré
square

Cet encrier est plein.
This inkwell is full.

Cet encrier est vide.
This inkwell is empty.

Ce livre est ouvert.
This book is open.

La mappemonde est ronde.
The globe is round.

– I'm so happy Li'l Davy's going to school!

– At last he's going to learn something…

– And this is a bear track… Has everyone understood?

l'heure • time

Cette aiguille indique les minutes.
This hand shows the minutes.

Cette aiguille indique les heures.
This hand shows the hours.

Le coucou est à l'heure.
The cuckoo clock is on time.

La montre de Dingo retarde.
Goofy's watch is slow.

la montre
watch

le réveil
alarm clock

Le réveil avance.
The alarm clock is fast.

Cette aiguille indique les secondes.
This hand shows the seconds.

Mickey remonte le réveil ; il sonnera demain matin à huit heures.
Mickey is winding the alarm clock; it will go off tomorrow morning at eight o'clock.

– Sale
– What a lovely cuckoo clock! I'm so happy I bought it!
– Good luck!

– Now, what time is it?

– It's two o'clock! My cuckoo clock is ringing!

les gens • people

la famille • the family

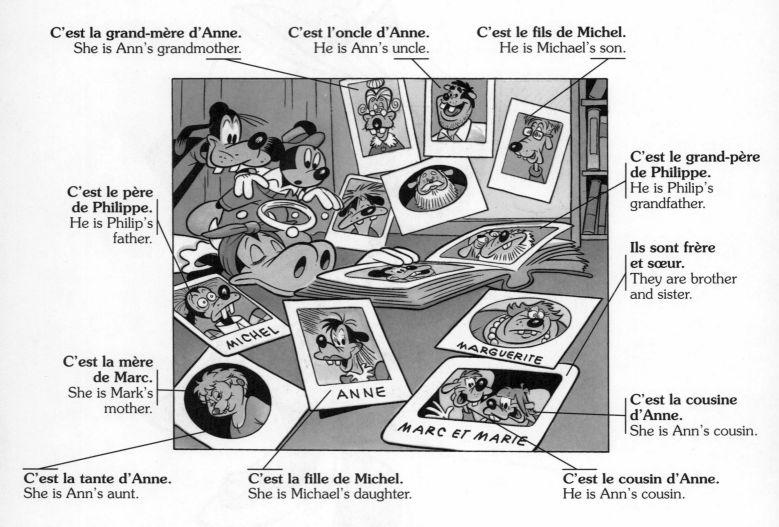

C'est la grand-mère d'Anne.
She is Ann's grandmother.

C'est l'oncle d'Anne.
He is Ann's uncle.

C'est le fils de Michel.
He is Michael's son.

C'est le grand-père de Philippe.
He is Philip's grandfather.

C'est le père de Philippe.
He is Philip's father.

Ils sont frère et sœur.
They are brother and sister.

C'est la mère de Marc.
She is Mark's mother.

C'est la cousine d'Anne.
She is Ann's cousin.

C'est la tante d'Anne.
She is Ann's aunt.

C'est la fille de Michel.
She is Michael's daughter.

C'est le cousin d'Anne.
He is Ann's cousin.

Michel est le mari de Marguerite.
Michael is Margaret's husband.

Marguerite est la femme de Michel.
Margaret is Michael's wife.

– See that? She cleans up really well!
– What a mess!

– Crash!

– I never thought you could be afraid of my family…

34

les personnes • people

la femme
woman

Il est heureux.
He is happy.

Elle est jeune.
She is young.

l'homme
man

la fille
girl

le bébé
baby

P'tit David est un garçon.
Li'l Davy is a boy.

La maman porte son bébé dans les bras.
The mother is holding her baby in her arms.

Elle a deux enfants.
She has two children.

– You think you can do it?
– Of course! Come and get him in half an hour.

– I'm warning you…
– Now… Now…

– But… But…
– I hate getting my hair cut!

l'aspect physique • appearance

Il est vieux.
He is old.

Il est gros.
He is fat.

Il est laid.
He is ugly.

Il est grand.
He is tall.

Il est maigre.
He is thin.

Il est fort.
He is strong.

Il est petit.
He is small.

Dingo est plus grand que Mickey.
Goofy is taller than Mickey.

Mickey est plus petit que Dingo.
Mickey is smaller than Goofy.

Jean est plus gros que Dingo.
John is fatter than Goofy.

– Mickey, do you need an orange squeezer?
– Oh yes, thanks!

– An orange squeezer would be very useful.

– That's really nice of you, Mickey! My cousin was out of work!

la chevelure • hair

Il a les cheveux courts.
He has short hair.

la queue de cheval
ponytail

la frange
fringe

la moustache
moustache

Elle est blonde.
She is blonde.

Il est brun.
He is dark.

la tresse
plait

la barbe
beard

la barrette
slide

Il est barbu et il a les cheveux raides.
He has a beard and straight hair.

La petite fille est rousse.
The little girl is red-haired.

Elle a les cheveux longs.
She has long hair.

– Mickey, could you pick up my
niece's babysitter?
– Yes...

– You don't mind if I bring my records?

– I'm going to get them to pull over; they look suspicious!

la personnalité • personality

Mickey est surpris.
Mickey is surprised.

P'tit David est poli.
Li'l Davy is polite.

Dingo est content.
Goofy is happy.

Elle est célèbre.
She is famous.

Dingo est pauvre.
Goofy is poor.

Miss Latour est riche.
Miss Latour is rich.

Mickey est gentil !
Mickey is nice!

– I'm going hunting!
– OK! But don't bring back an Indian chief or a bear like you usually do…

– Go ahead and laugh, but he often can give you a nasty surprise!

– Later
– I hope you don't mind…
I invited…
– No! Certainly not!

– I'm really sorry, Miss Latour!
– It's all right, Li'l Davy!
– I should have kept my mouth shut…

les vêtements (1) • clothes (1)

le chemisier
blouse

Elle porte une jolie robe longue.
She is wearing a lovely evening dress.

la veste
jacket

le nœud papillon
bow tie

le jupon
petticoat

la cravate
tie

Elle est très élégante.
She looks very smart.

le collant
tights

la robe
dress

Minnie s'est maquillée.
Minnie is wearing make-up.

Mickey a un costume neuf.
Mickey has a new suit.

– Are you going to the dance tonight?
– No, unless I find an old-fashioned girl.

– Did Goofy find a girl he liked?

– Yes! He never does things by halves!

les vêtements (2) • clothes (2)

le chapeau
hat

le portemanteau
coatstand

la casquette
cap

le manteau
coat

l'imperméable
raincoat

le pantalon
trousers

la jupe
skirt

Sa veste est trop large.
His jacket is too big.

le jean
jeans

Le pantalon de Mickey est trop court.
Mickey's trousers are too short.

Minnie va s'habiller.
Minnie is going to get dressed.

– You're really going to wear those this evening?
– Yes! Bullfighter trousers are all the rage now.

– That evening…
– My first guest… I hope it's Mickey!

– Here we are!

les vêtements (3) • clothes (3)

la penderie
wardrobe

le tee-shirt
tee-shirt

le pull-over
pullover

la chemise
shirt

la ceinture
belt

les chaussons
slippers

le tiroir
drawer

les chaussettes
socks

Il y a beaucoup de vêtements dans la penderie.
There are a lot of clothes in the wardrobe.

Il a accroché son bonnet au portemanteau.
He has hung his cap on the peg.

GRÂCE À CE PRODUIT, IL N'Y AURA PLUS DE MITES...

– Thanks to this spray, there'll be no more moths...

ELLES NE SAVENT PAS CE QUI LES ATTEND...

– They'll never know what hit them...

PLUS TARD...

J'AVAIS OUBLIÉ MON PLUS BEAU COSTUME !

– Later...
– I've forgotten my best suit!

les chaussures · shoes

Sa botte est trouée.
There is a hole in his boot.

Il a mal au pied.
His foot hurts.

le tennis
tennis shoe

le lacet
shoelace

le talon
heel

l'escarpin
court shoe

la botte
boot

la bottine
ankle boot

Les chaussures de Dingo sont trop grandes.
Goofy's shoes are too big.

TU AVAIS DIT QUE TU N'IRAIS PLUS AU BAL...

OUI... MAIS J'AI QUAND MÊME ENVIE DE M'AMU-SER...

ÇA, C'EST BIZARRE...

ET ALORS, QU'EST-CE QUE ÇA PEUT TE FAIRE?

JE NE SUPPORTAIS PLUS DE ME FAIRE MARCHER SUR LES PIEDS.

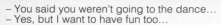

– You said you weren't going to the dance…
– Yes, but I want to have fun too…

– That's strange…
– What's it to you?

– I couldn't stand people stepping on my feet anymore.

les bijoux • jewellery

la bague
ring

Cette bague en or brille.
This gold ring glitters.

la boucle d'oreille
earring

l'émeraude
emerald

la perle
bead

le collier
necklace

le bracelet
bracelet

Le collier de Minnie s'est cassé.
Minnie's necklace broke.

la broche
brooch

le rubis
ruby

Les perles ont roulé sur le sol.
The beads rolled on the floor.

Les émeraudes et les rubis sont des pierres précieuses.
Emeralds and rubies are precious stones.

– Mickey! My beads…!
– I'll pick them up for you!

– Gosh! There are a lot of them!

– There… I think I've got them all…

– Everyone else went home long ago!

le corps humain • the human body

les parties du corps (1) • parts of the body (1)

la tête
head

Il fronce les sourcils.
He is frowning.

l'épaule
shoulder

le cou
neck

les fesses
bottom

le ventre
stomach

le dos
back

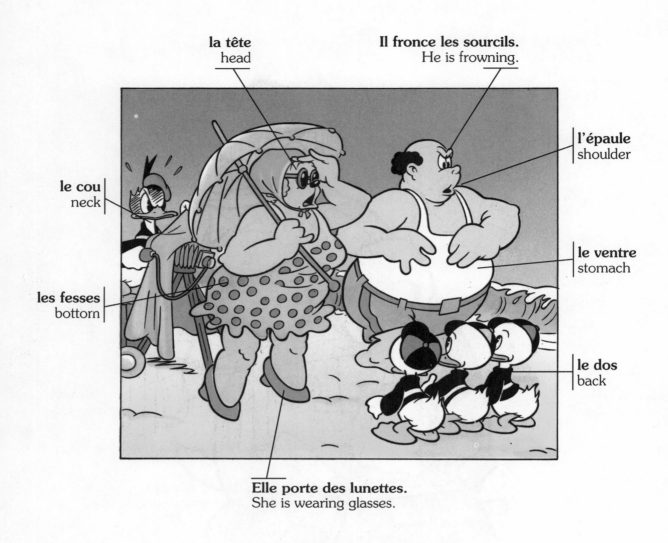

Elle porte des lunettes.
She is wearing glasses.

La dame tourne le dos à Donald.
The lady is turning her back on Donald.

– Hey, you! Can't you see I'm taking a photo?

– Oh, Oscar!

les parties du corps (2) • parts of the body (2)

Il croise les bras.
His arms are crossed.

Le masseur est debout.
The masseur is standing up.

la jambe
leg

le bras
arm

le doigt
finger

le pied
foot

le coude
elbow

Il porte des sandales.
He is wearing sandals.

la main
hand

le doigt de pied
toe

le genou
knee

Donald est allongé.
Donald is lying down.

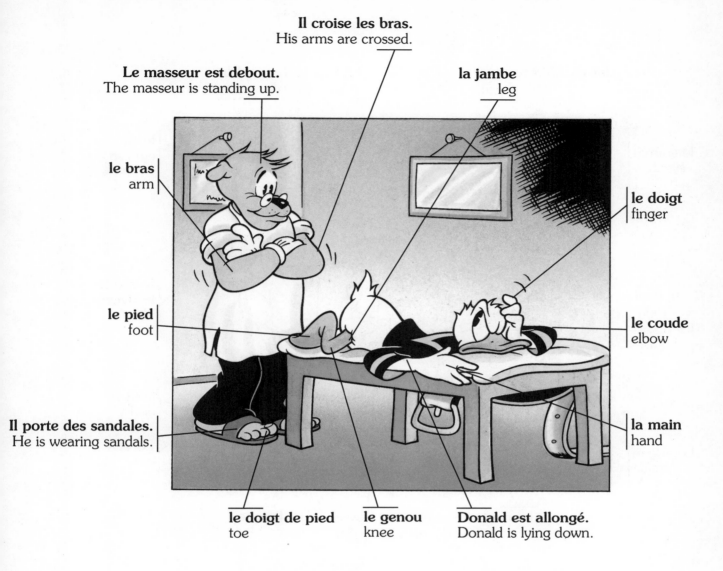

Le masseur a les bras musclés.
The masseur's arms are well-muscled.

Donald se fait masser une fois par semaine.
Donald has a massage once a week.

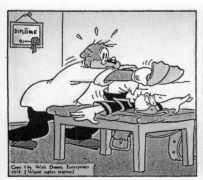

– Diploma

– Crack

– That'll be one dollar, sir!

le visage • the face

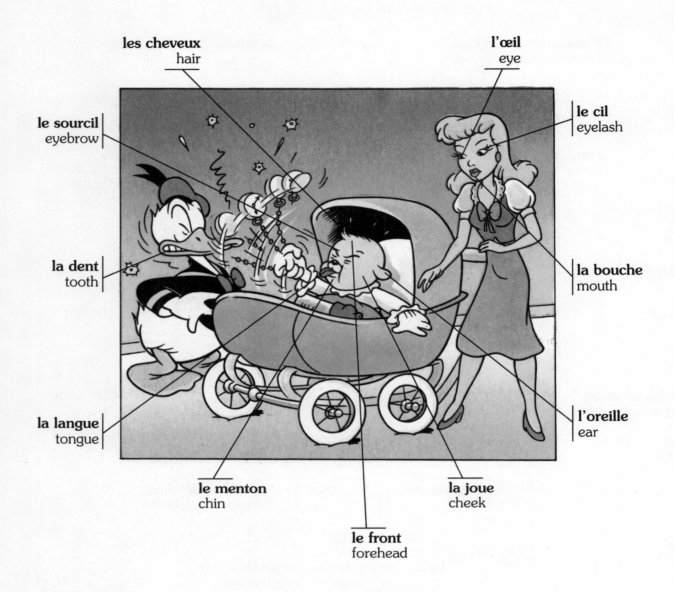

les cheveux
hair

l'œil
eye

le sourcil
eyebrow

le cil
eyelash

la dent
tooth

la bouche
mouth

la langue
tongue

l'oreille
ear

le menton
chin

la joue
cheek

le front
forehead

Le bébé tire la langue.
The baby is sticking out his tongue.

– Oh! Aren't you cute!
Cootchy, cootchy coo!

– Shh!
– Boohoo!

– Look! The watch is
going tick-tock!

la santé • health

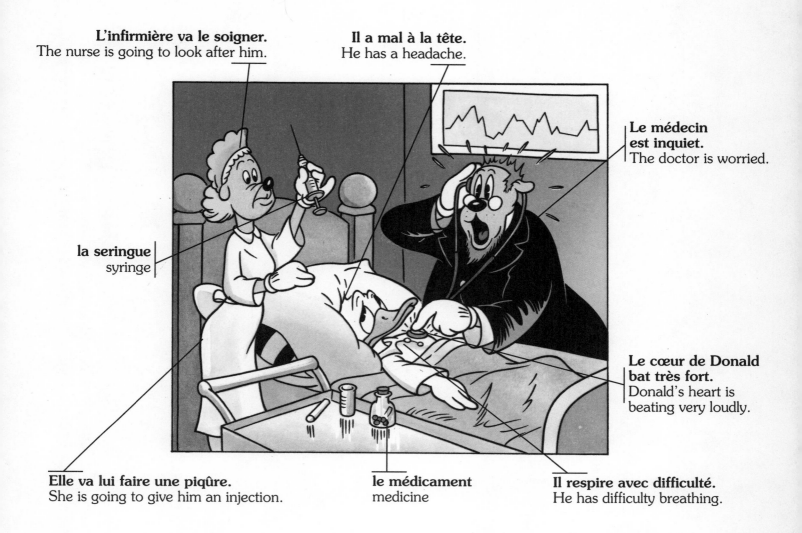

L'infirmière va le soigner.
The nurse is going to look after him.

Il a mal à la tête.
He has a headache.

Le médecin est inquiet.
The doctor is worried.

la seringue
syringe

Le cœur de Donald bat très fort.
Donald's heart is beating very loudly.

Elle va lui faire une piqûre.
She is going to give him an injection.

le médicament
medicine

Il respire avec difficulté.
He has difficulty breathing.

On l'a transporté à l'hôpital en ambulance.
He was brought to the hospital by ambulance.

Donald va peut-être mourir.
Perhaps Donald will die.

– I'll pretend to be sick…

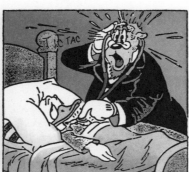

– Tick tock

– Ha ha! That fooled him!

– Ambulance

la nourriture • food

les légumes • vegetables

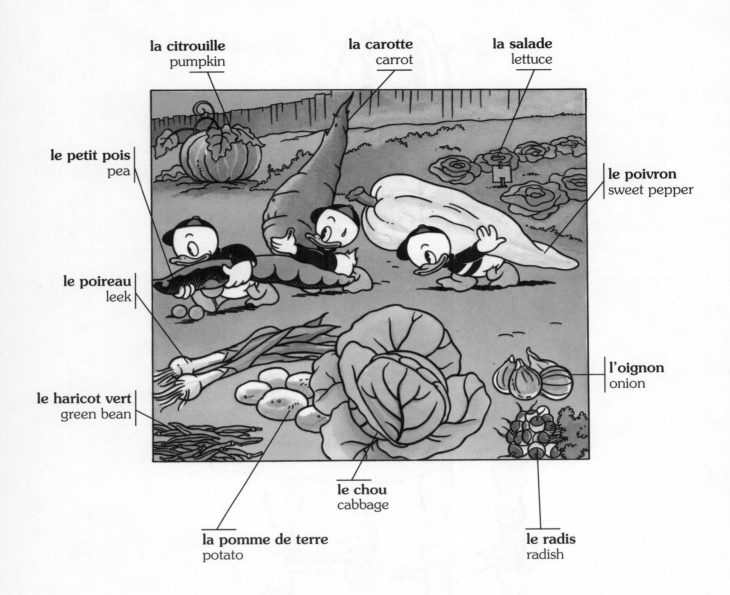

la citrouille
pumpkin

la carotte
carrot

la salade
lettuce

le petit pois
pea

le poivron
sweet pepper

le poireau
leek

l'oignon
onion

le haricot vert
green bean

le chou
cabbage

le radis
radish

la pomme de terre
potato

– We bought some…
– … magic fertilizer.
– Magic fertilizer
– You know, it's rain and work that make plants grow…

– It's raining! I bet everything will have grown by tomorrow!

– Morning
– I can't wait to see…

– There! I told you everything would have…
– … grown!

les fruits • fruit

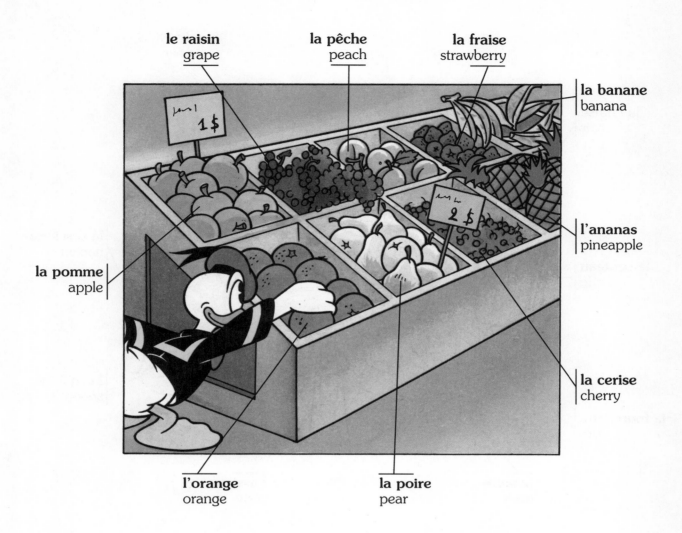

le raisin
grape

la pêche
peach

la fraise
strawberry

la banane
banana

la pomme
apple

l'ananas
pineapple

la cerise
cherry

l'orange
orange

la poire
pear

Les fruits sont mûrs.
The fruit is ripe.

La pêche est un fruit.
A peach is a piece of fruit.

– Have you seen the lovely fruit?

– Do you want any more?

la table • the table

la chaise
chair

le sel
salt

le poivre
pepper

le couteau
knife

la serviette
napkin

la fourchette
fork

la cuillère
spoon

le verre
glass

l'assiette
plate

Donald porte un plat.
Donald is holding a dish.

Gontran a toujours faim et soif.
Gladstone is always hungry and thirsty.

– There! I hope that's enough!

– Oh dear! He's so greedy! I hope he leaves me something to eat…

– What? There's nothing left but the…

– … bones?

le petit déjeuner · breakfast

Donald boit du café.
Donald is drinking coffee.

la tasse
cup

le lait
milk

les céréales
cereal

l'œuf
egg

la confiture
jam

le beurre
butter

la théière
teapot

la cafetière
coffee-pot

le miel
honey

le sucre
sugar

le pain
bread

Il a préparé du thé.
He has got tea ready.

Les neveux ne sont pas encore levés.
The nephews are not up yet.

– This coffee has no sugar in it…

– This sugar dispenser really isn't very practical…

– I've a solution!

le déjeuner • lunch

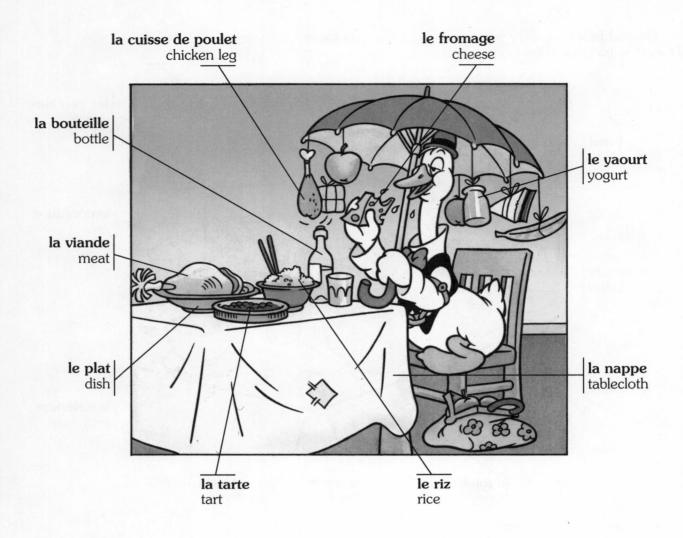

la cuisse de poulet
chicken leg

le fromage
cheese

la bouteille
bottle

le yaourt
yogurt

la viande
meat

le plat
dish

la nappe
tablecloth

la tarte
tart

le riz
rice

Gontran mange beaucoup.
Gladstone eats a lot.

Le fromage est délicieux.
The cheese is delicious.

– You see? There's nothing to eat!

– It worked! He's going back to his house!

– Plop!

le dîner • dinner

Gontran a vidé le réfrigérateur.
Gladstone has emptied the fridge.

La soupe est brûlante.
The soup is boiling hot.

Donald est en colère.
Donald is angry.

l'eau
water

la poêle
frying pan

le poisson
fish

la soupière
soup tureen

la louche
ladle

la soupe
soup

Gontran n'est pas un vrai somnambule !
Gladstone is not a real sleepwalker!

Il aime le poisson.
He likes fish.

– Where is he going?

– Into the kitchen?

la nature • nature

la forêt • the forest

le nid
nest

la branche
branch

la feuille
leaf

l'arbre
tree

Les feuilles tombent.
The leaves are falling.

le tronc
trunk

l'écureuil
squirrel

la châtaigne
chestnut

l'herbe
grass

Mickey a ramassé des champignons.
Mickey has been picking mushrooms.

C'est l'automne.
It is autumn.

Ils sont dans une clairière.
They are in a clearing.

– What will we eat today, boys?
– How about an eagle-egg omelet?
– An eagle-egg omelet?

– It's delicious! And I know just where to find the eggs in the forest!

– A little later…
– Don't wait for me! I may be a little late!

la montagne • the mountains

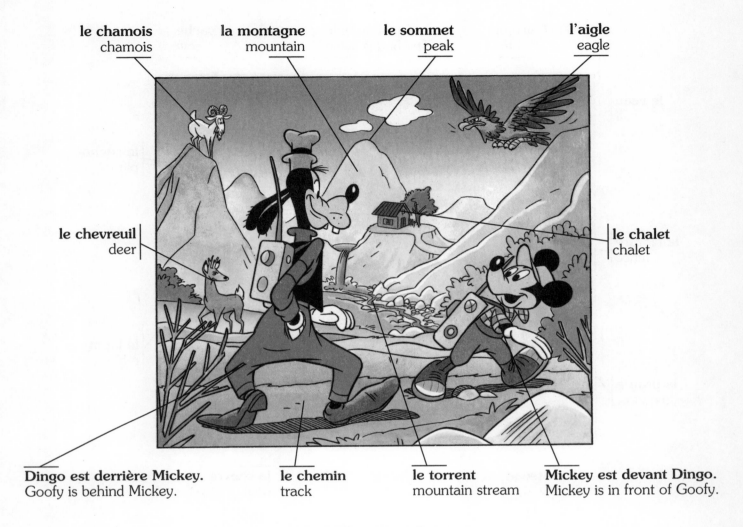

le chamois — chamois

la montagne — mountain

le sommet — peak

l'aigle — eagle

le chevreuil — deer

le chalet — chalet

Dingo est derrière Mickey.
Goofy is behind Mickey.

le chemin
track

le torrent
mountain stream

Mickey est devant Dingo.
Mickey is in front of Goofy.

La vallée est en bas.
The valley is below.

Le sommet est en haut.
The peak is above.

– It's fun collecting birds' eggs for the museum...
– Let's keep in touch on the walkie-talkie!

– Later...
– Bzzz Bzzz
– I wonder what Goofy wants...

– Have you found anything?
– No, I'm the one who's been found!

la campagne • the countryside

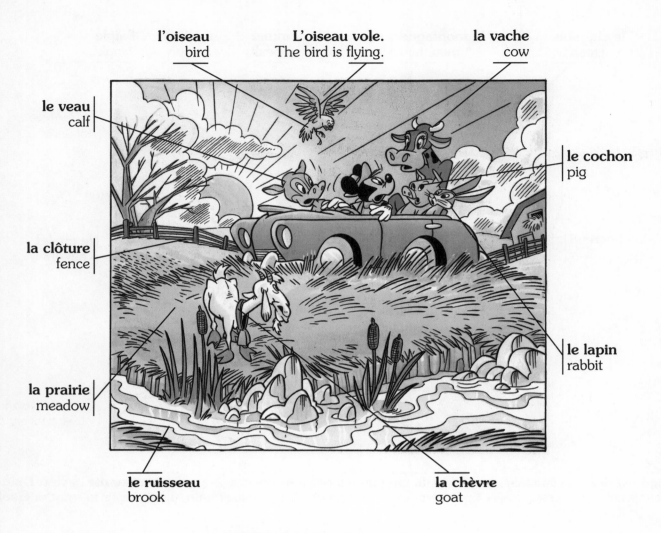

l'oiseau
bird

L'oiseau vole.
The bird is flying.

la vache
cow

le veau
calf

le cochon
pig

la clôture
fence

le lapin
rabbit

la prairie
meadow

le ruisseau
brook

la chèvre
goat

Le soleil se lève : il est très tôt.
The sun is rising: it is very early.

Quel beau paysage !
What a beautiful landscape!

– It's too dangerous to drive in this fog! I'll pull over and wait.

– Morning...
– I fell asleep! At last the fog's lifted...

– One thing is certain, it was very foggy!

les fleurs • flowers

la rose
rose

l'œillet
carnation

le bouquet
bouquet

la tulipe
tulip

l'abeille
bee

la tige
stem

Ça sent bon !
What a lovely smell!

Cette fleur est fanée.
This flower has wilted.

les pétales
petals

la marguerite
daisy

Il n'y a que des fleurs, il n'y a pas de plantes vertes.
There are only flowers here; there are no green plants.

– Oh! I'm sorry!
– Florist

– Minnie, just let me explain!

la rivière • the river

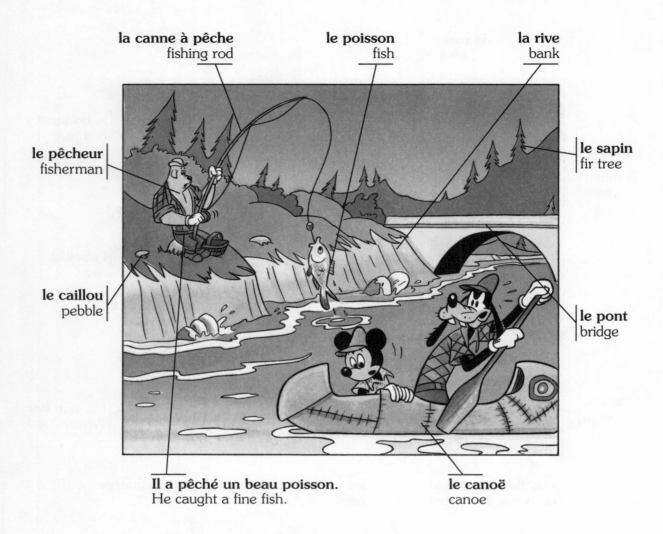

la canne à pêche
fishing rod

le poisson
fish

la rive
bank

le pêcheur
fisherman

le sapin
fir tree

le caillou
pebble

le pont
bridge

Il a pêché un beau poisson.
He caught a fine fish.

le canoë
canoe

La rivière est profonde.
The river is deep.

L'eau coule sous le pont.
The water is flowing under the bridge.

– It's a real canoe… I built it just like the Indians do!
– It doesn't look very sturdy…

– We're sinking!
– No we aren't! In a minute, we'll be in the middle
of the river!

– Come back, Goofy! Come back!

la mer • the sea

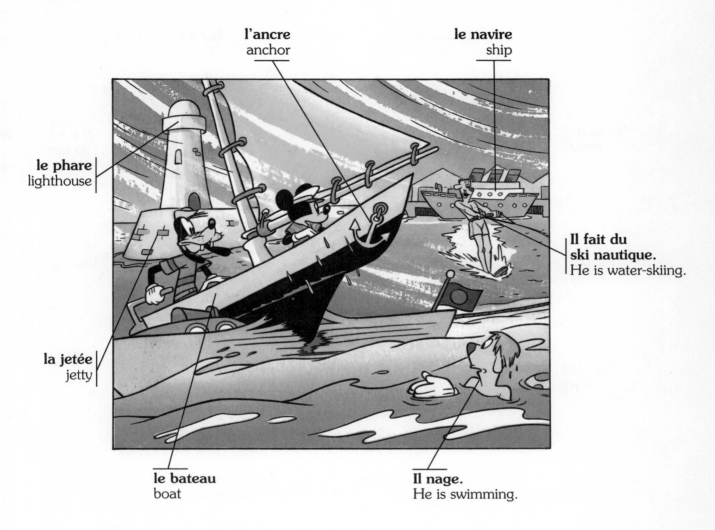

l'ancre
anchor

le navire
ship

le phare
lighthouse

Il fait du
ski nautique.
He is water-skiing.

la jetée
jetty

le bateau
boat

Il nage.
He is swimming.

Il y a un navire dans le port.
There is a ship in the harbour.

Le vent souffle.
The wind is blowing.

– Get the sail down! There's too much wind!
– I'm trying!

– Mickey!
– I can't do it!

– Police
– I don't suppose you'd be interested in an explanation…

le ciel • the sky

la soucoupe volante
flying saucer

la lune
moon

le nuage
cloud

Il y a un croissant de lune.
There is a crescent moon.

l'avion
aeroplane

la chouette
owl

l'étoile
star

Les étoiles brillent dans le ciel.
The stars are shining in the sky.

La soucoupe volante traverse les airs.
The flying saucer is crossing the sky.

La nuit est agitée.
It is a hectic night.

– I've got an idea! I'm going to make my kite just like a seagull!
– I see…

– There we are! I'm flying away like a… Aaah!

– OK, now explain how I get back down!

l'orage • the storm

Dingo s'abrite à l'intérieur de la maison.
Goofy is sheltering inside the house.

l'éclair
lightning

le parapluie
umbrella

l'imperméable
raincoat

la pluie
rain

la flaque
puddle

Les chaussures de Mickey sont mouillées.
Mickey's shoes are wet.

Il y a du vent !
It is windy!

On entend le tonnerre.
Thunder can be heard.

– I'm going to hang up my barometer and see what the weather will be… Oops!

– It's stuck!
– Fine
– Rain

– I think I did something silly…

la ferme • the farm

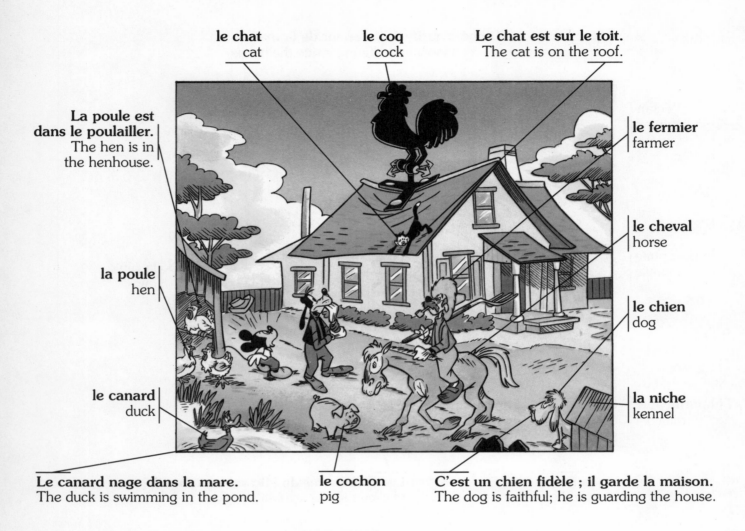

le chat
cat

le coq
cock

Le chat est sur le toit.
The cat is on the roof.

La poule est dans le poulailler.
The hen is in the henhouse.

le fermier
farmer

le cheval
horse

la poule
hen

le chien
dog

le canard
duck

la niche
kennel

Le canard nage dans la mare.
The duck is swimming in the pond.

le cochon
pig

C'est un chien fidèle ; il garde la maison.
The dog is faithful; he is guarding the house.

Combien y a-t-il d'animaux ?
How many animals are there?

Le fermier monte à cheval.
The farmer is riding his horse.

– I've decided to put a weathercock on my roof!
– That's a good idea!

– A few days later…
– I'm going to see Goofy… His weathercock must be ready by now…

– I think I must have got the instructions wrong…

les animaux sauvages • wild animals

la girafe
giraffe

l'hippopotame
hippopotamus

le singe
monkey

Le zèbre court vite.
The zebra is running quickly.

l'éléphant
elephant

Mickey a peur des animaux sauvages.
Mickey is afraid of wild animals.

le lion
lion

le serpent
snake

le crocodile
crocodile

Attention ! Le lion a l'air méchant.
Watch out! The lion looks cross.

La girafe a un long cou.
The giraffe has a long neck.

– But, Minnie… I didn't want my sitting-room papered.
– Come and see how amazing these new wallpapers are!

– See! It looks like a real garden! Do you like it?
– Yes… I almost thought…

– Wait and see what I have chosen for your sitting-room!…

– Later

les loisirs • leisure

l'aéroport • the airport

Arrivées
Arrivals

Cet avion décolle.
This plane is taking off.

Départs
Departures

l'avion
aeroplane

le hangar
hangar

Cet avion atterrit.
This plane is landing.

l'hôtesse de l'air
air hostess

le douanier
customs officer

la douane
customs

Une femme montre son passeport au douanier.
A woman is showing her passport to the customs officer.

– You can land the plane today...
– But... But...

– That's it! Go easy now!

– Bravo! I couldn't have done better!
– Help!

la plage • the beach

le palmier
palm tree

Le soleil brille.
The sun is shining.

Il fait un château de sable.
He is building a sand castle.

le parasol
beach umbrella

les lunettes de soleil
sunglasses

le maillot de bain
bathing suit

la bouée
rubber ring

les coquillages
shells

le sable
sand

Elle est bronzée.
She is sun-tanned.

Ils sont en vacances.
They are on holiday.

Il fait beau, c'est l'été.
The weather is fine; it is summer.

– There're a lot of people here!...

– Where can I sit?

le camping · camping

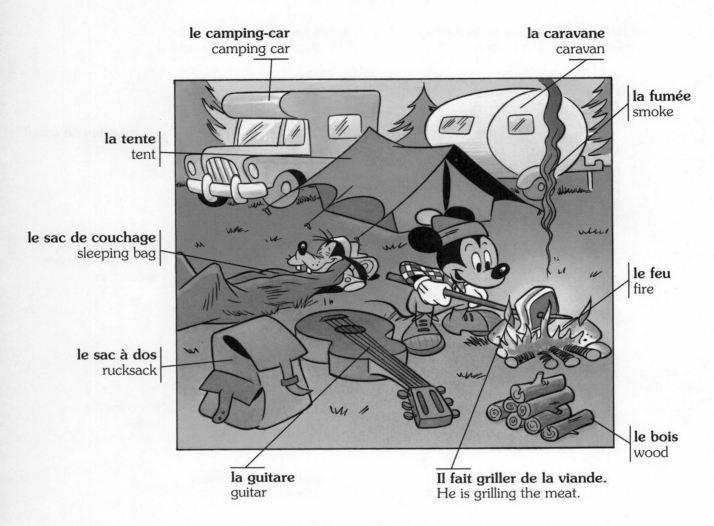

le camping-car
camping car

la caravane
caravan

la fumée
smoke

la tente
tent

le sac de couchage
sleeping bag

le sac à dos
rucksack

le feu
fire

le bois
wood

la guitare
guitar

Il fait griller de la viande.
He is grilling the meat.

Mickey se réchauffe auprès du feu.
Mickey is warming himself beside the fire.

Mickey adore faire du camping.
Mickey loves camping.

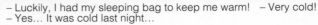

– Well, Goofy, are you glad you slept in the great outdoors?
– Yes…

– Luckily, I had my sleeping bag to keep me warm!
– Yes… It was cold last night…

– Very cold!

les jouets et les jeux • toys and games

le ballon
ball

le mobile
mobile

le domino
domino

l'ours en peluche
teddy bear

le jeu de dames
checkers

le jeu d'échecs
chess

le damier
draught-board

le puzzle
puzzle

la poupée
doll

le cube
building block

Le puzzle n'est pas fini.
The puzzle is not finished.

Il y a du désordre dans la salle de jeux.
The playroom is untidy.

La poupée s'appelle Caroline.
The doll's name is Caroline.

– Come on, Morty! It's bedtime!
– I want to keep playing, Mickey!

– You go to bed!
– I was having such fun with you!

– This game of dominos was so boring! I prefer Morty's toys!
– Me too!

le zoo • the zoo

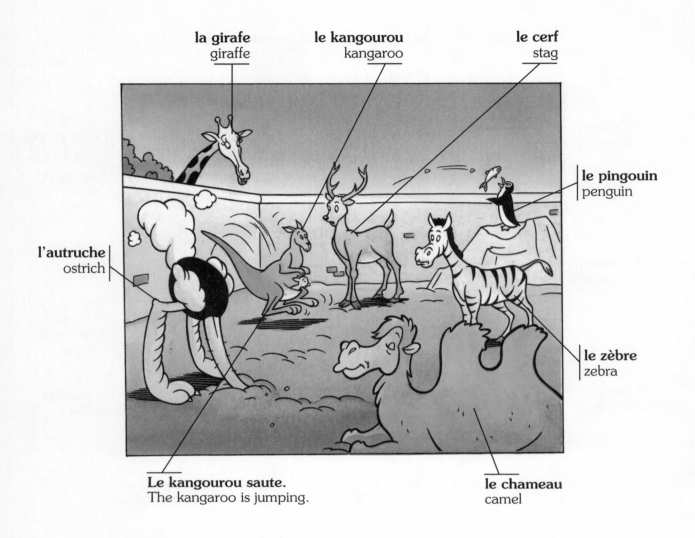

la girafe
giraffe

le kangourou
kangaroo

le cerf
stag

le pingouin
penguin

l'autruche
ostrich

le zèbre
zebra

Le kangourou saute.
The kangaroo is jumping.

le chameau
camel

Le pingouin attrape un poisson.
The penguin is catching a fish.

L'autruche se cache.
The ostrich is hiding.

– What are you talking about?
My ostrich is a bad influence on
the other animals?

– O.K. I'll go to the zoo and see what's
happening.

la peinture • painting

le crayon pencil

la règle ruler

la gomme rubber

Ce tableau est un chef-d'œuvre ! This painting is a masterpiece!

Il y a des taches de peinture sur son tablier. There are paint stains on his smock.

la toile canvas

la palette palette

le tube de peinture tube of paint

le papier paper

le pinceau paint brush

L'artiste peint bien.
The artist paints well.

Il a fait le portrait de Donald.
He has painted Donald's portrait.

– It's really not expensive…
– I've got to eat! I'm a poor starving artist!
– Portraits painted $ 2

la musique • music

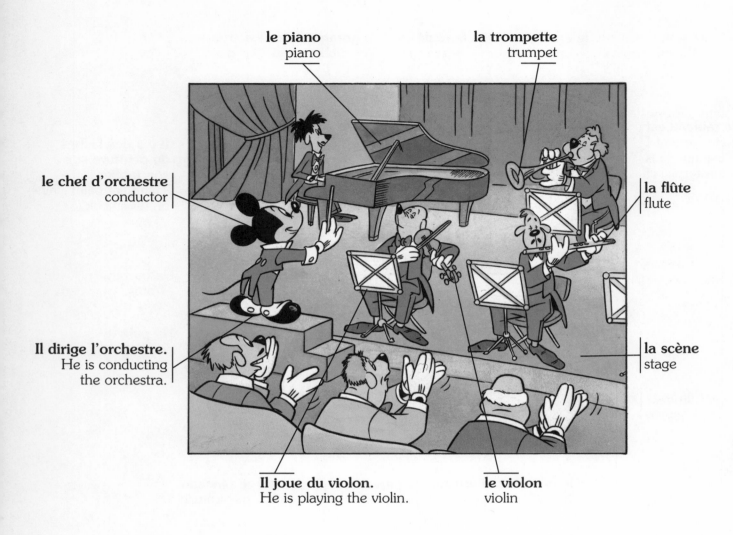

le piano
piano

la trompette
trumpet

le chef d'orchestre
conductor

la flûte
flute

Il dirige l'orchestre.
He is conducting
the orchestra.

la scène
stage

Il joue du violon.
He is playing the violin.

le violon
violin

Le public applaudit.
The audience is clapping.

– I didn't know you were giving a concert here.
– Oh really?
– Stage door

le concert • the concert

C'est un bon musicien.
He is a good musician.

le chanteur
singer

la guitare électrique
electric guitar

le saxophone
saxophone

le micro
microphone

la batterie
drums

le synthétiseur
synthesizer

Il chante faux.
He is singing out of tune.

Tout le monde danse.
Everybody is dancing.

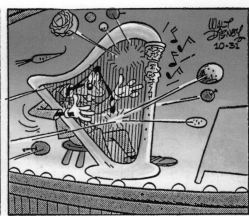

– Music competition

– Later
– A harp?
– Yes! I changed my instrument!

le cinéma • the cinema

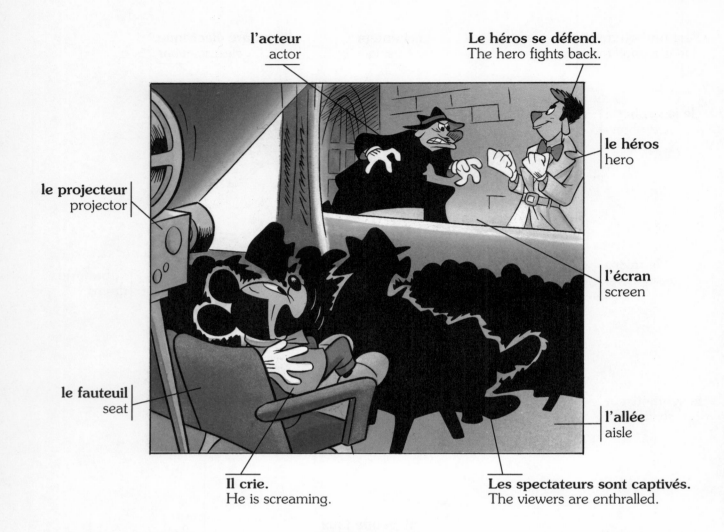

l'acteur
actor

Le héros se défend.
The hero fights back.

le héros
hero

le projecteur
projector

l'écran
screen

le fauteuil
seat

l'allée
aisle

Il crie.
He is screaming.

Les spectateurs sont captivés.
The viewers are enthralled.

Quel suspense !
How exciting!

Le film est effrayant.
The film is scary.

– I just love horror films… I can't see the screen…

– Excuse me, could you take your hat off?

– Arrgh!

le parc • the park

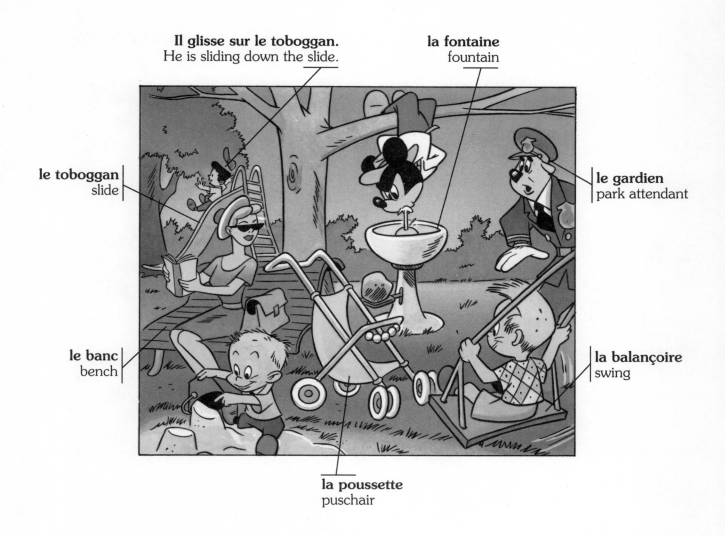

Il glisse sur le toboggan.
He is sliding down the slide.

la fontaine
fountain

le toboggan
slide

le gardien
park attendant

le banc
bench

la balançoire
swing

la poussette
puschair

– I'm thirsty!

les sports • sport

le stade • the stadium

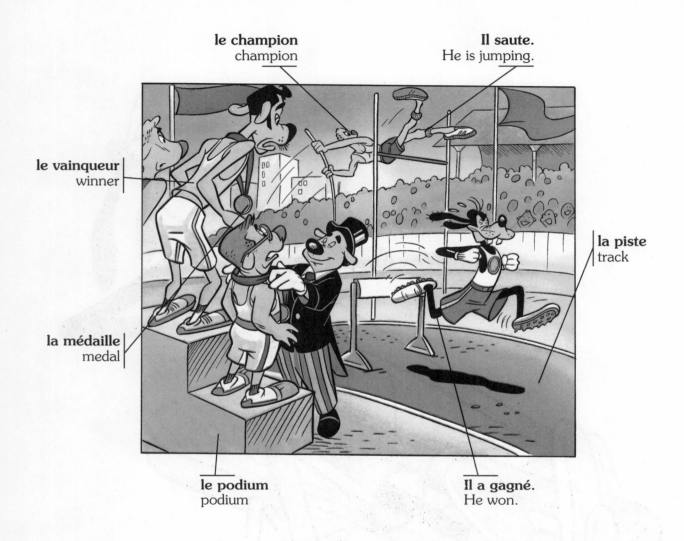

le champion
champion

Il saute.
He is jumping.

le vainqueur
winner

la piste
track

la médaille
medal

le podium
podium

Il a gagné.
He won.

Dingo court.
Goofy is running.

– Forget the other athletes. Concentrate on the race: close your eyes and run!
– You can depend on me!

– Goofy!
– Finish

– I think I can open my eyes now…

l'équipement • sportsgear

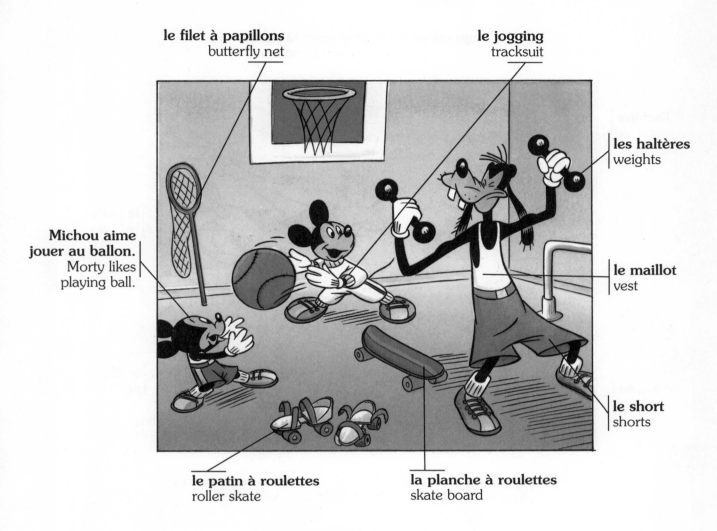

le filet à papillons
butterfly net

le jogging
tracksuit

les haltères
weights

**Michou aime
jouer au ballon.**
Morty likes
playing ball.

le maillot
vest

le short
shorts

le patin à roulettes
roller skate

la planche à roulettes
skate board

Ils sont au gymnase.
They are in the gym.

Minnie préfère la gymnastique.
Minnie prefers gymnastics.

– I must get a little exercise.

– It really is strong for a butterfly!

– You've given up chasing butterflies?
– Yes, it's too dangerous!

le tennis de table • table tennis

Dingo est en train de gagner la partie.
Goofy is winning the match.

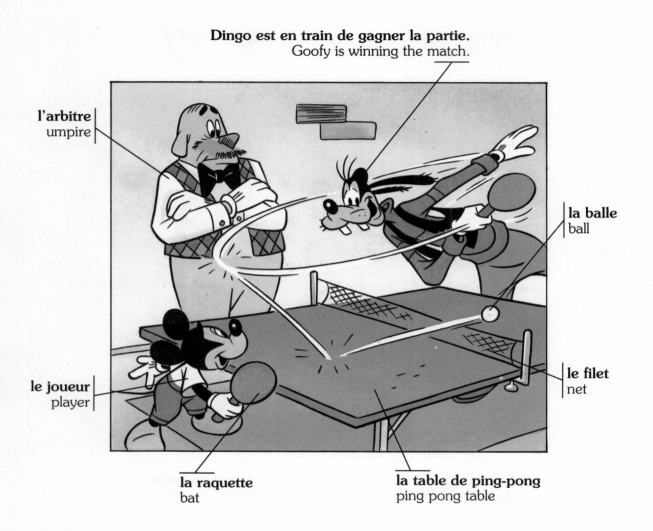

l'arbitre
umpire

la balle
ball

le joueur
player

le filet
net

la raquette
bat

la table de ping-pong
ping pong table

C'est la balle de match.
It is the match point.

– You play well Goofy, but you wave your arms a lot!
– I'm so excited by the game that I can't keep still.

le ski • skiing

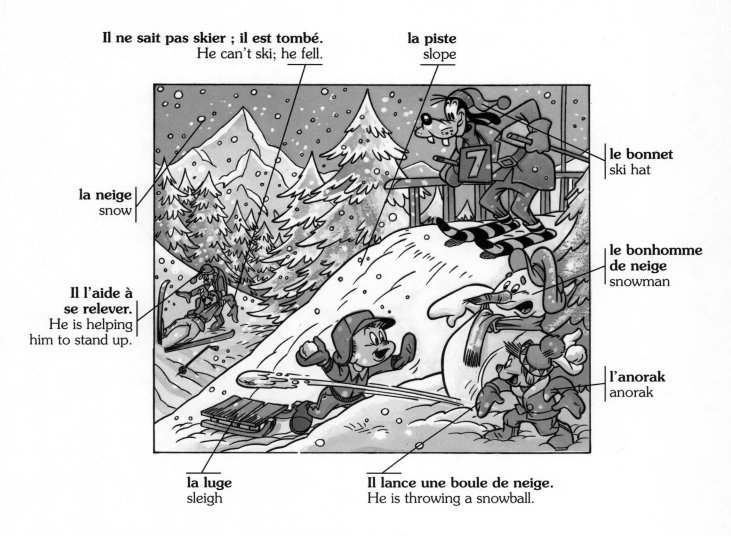

Il ne sait pas skier ; il est tombé.
He can't ski; he fell.

la piste
slope

le bonnet
ski hat

la neige
snow

le bonhomme de neige
snowman

Il l'aide à se relever.
He is helping him to stand up.

l'anorak
anorak

la luge
sleigh

Il lance une boule de neige.
He is throwing a snowball.

Il neige, c'est l'hiver.
It is snowing; it is winter.

Il fait froid.
It is cold.

– What a pity you can't be in the race!
– I can't afford skis…

– Starch

– I should have thought of this long ago!

la fête • holidays

la fête de Noël • Christmas

la boule
ball

le père Noël
Father Christmas

l'arbre de Noël
Christmas tree

la cheminée
fireplace

la guirlande
garland

la bûche
log

Riri admire son cadeau.
Dewey is admiring his present.

Le père Noël est passé.
Father Christmas has come.

– Here's the turkey, Donald!

– Breast or leg?

le pique-nique • the picnic

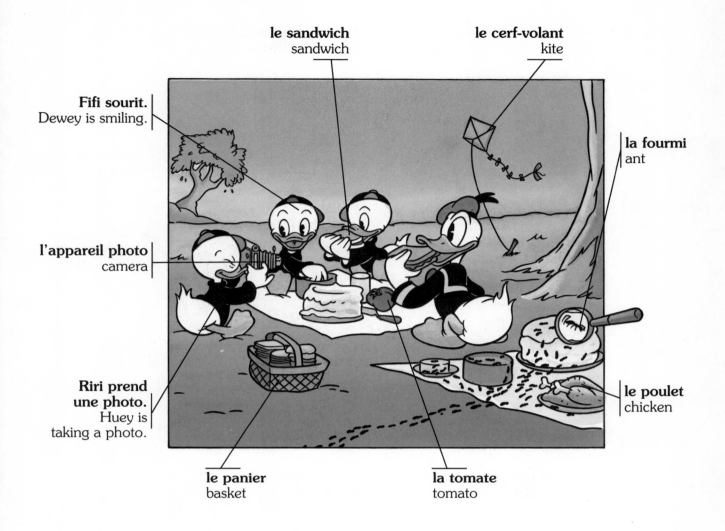

le sandwich
sandwich

le cerf-volant
kite

Fifi sourit.
Dewey is smiling.

la fourmi
ant

l'appareil photo
camera

**Riri prend
une photo.**
Huey is
taking a photo.

le poulet
chicken

le panier
basket

la tomate
tomato

C'est un repas froid.
It is a cold meal.

C'est dimanche, tout le monde pique-nique, même les fourmis !
It is Sunday; everyone is having a picnic, even the ants!

l'anniversaire • the birthday party

Il lui donne un bonbon.
He is giving him a sweet.

Il offre un cadeau à Loulou.
He is giving Louie a present.

le jus d'orange
orange juice

le gâteau d'anniversaire
birthday cake

la limonade
lemonade

la tablette de chocolat
bar of chocolate

la sucette
lollipop

Fifi souffle les bougies du gâteau.
Huey is blowing out the candles on the cake.

C'est l'anniversaire des neveux.
It is the nephews' birthday.

– Our guests haven't come yet…
– … for our birthday party.
– May we eat the ice cream?
– No, wait a little bit longer!

– And now…
– … may we…
– … eat it?
– Okay! You can!

– But first of all, you should get changed…

– Invitation.

le cirque • the circus

l'écuyère
rider

le spectateur
spectator

la cage
cage

la piste
ring

le clown
clown

le jongleur
juggler

le dompteur
tamer

C'est la fin du spectacle.
It is the end of the performance.

Les artistes défilent.
The performers are parading.

– It's a beautiful flat, on the first floor at the back.
– That won't do. I'm looking for a flat that looks onto the street.
– For rent

– I have to hurry!

– Second floor, overlooking the street… the rent is $ 500 per month.
– It doesn't matter! I'd like to look at it!

– The drawing room… Note this xivth century painting…

Annexes

French verbs conjugations

	-er Verbs	-ir Verbs	-re Verbs
Infinitive	chant-*er*	fin-*ir*	vend-*re*
Present	je chante tu chantes il chante nous chantons vous chantez ils chantent	je finis tu finis il finit nous finissons vous finissez ils finissent	je vends tu vends il vend nous vendons vous vendez ils vendent
Imperfect	je chantais tu chantais il chantait nous chantions vous chantiez ils chantaient	je finissais tu finissais il finissait nous finissions vous finissiez ils finissaient	je vendais tu vendais il vendait nous vendions vous vendiez ils vendaient
Past historic	je chantai tu chantas il chanta nous chantâmes vous chantâtes ils chantèrent	je finis tu finis il finit nous finîmes vous finîtes ils finirent	je vendis tu vendis il vendit nous vendîmes vous vendîtes ils vendirent
Future	je chanterai tu chanteras il chantera nous chanterons vous chanterez ils chanteront	je finirai tu finiras il finira nous finirons vous finirez ils finiront	je vendrai tu vendras il vendra nous vendrons vous vendrez ils vendront
Subjunctive	que je chante que tu chantes qu'il chante que nous chantions que vous chantiez qu'ils chantent	que je finisse que tu finisses qu'il finisse que nous finissions que vous finissiez qu'ils finissent	que je vende que tu vendes qu'il vende que nous vendions que vous vendiez qu'ils vendent
Imperative	chante chantons chantez	finis finissons finissez	vends vendons vendez
Present participle	chantant	finissant	vendant
Past participle	chanté	fini	vendu

Les nombres • Numerals

Les nombres cardinaux • Cardinal numbers

zéro	0	nought
un	1	one
deux	2	two
trois	3	three
quatre	4	four
cinq	5	five
six	6	six
sept	7	seven
huit	8	eight
neuf	9	nine
dix	10	ten

onze	11	eleven
douze	12	twelve
treize	13	thirteen
quatorze	14	fourteen
quinze	15	fifteen
seize	16	sixteen
dix-sept	17	seventeen
dix-huit	18	eighteen
dix-neuf	19	nineteen
vingt	20	twenty
vingt et un	21	twenty-one
vingt-deux	22	twenty-two
trente	30	thirty
quarante	40	forty
cinquante	50	fifty
soixante	60	sixty

soixante-dix	70	seventy
soixante-quinze	75	seventy-five
quatre-vingts	80	eighty
quatre-vingt-un	81	eighty-one
quatre-vingt-dix	90	ninety
quatre-vingt-onze	91	ninety-one
cent	100	a/one hundred
cent un	101	a hundred and one
cent deux	102	a hundred and two
cent cinquante	150	a hundred and fifty
deux cents	200	two hundred
deux cent un	201	two hundred and one
deux cent deux	202	two hundred and two
mille	1000	a/one thousand
mille un	1001	a thousand and one
mille deux	1002	a thousand and two
deux mille	2000	two thousand
un million	1000000	a/one million
deux millions	2000000	two million

Les nombres ordinaux
Ordinal numbers

premier	1er	1st	first
deuxième	2e	2nd	second
troisième	3e	3rd	third
quatrième	4e	4th	fourth
cinquième	5e	5th	fifth
sixième	6e	6th	sixth
septième	7e	7th	seventh
huitième	8e	8th	eighth
neuvième	9e	9th	ninth
dixième	10e	10th	tenth
onzième	11e	11th	eleventh
douzième	12e	12th	twelfth
treizième	13e	13th	thirteenth
quatorzième	14e	14th	fourteenth
quinzième	15e	15th	fifteenth
seizième	16e	16th	sixteenth
dix-septième	17e	17th	seventeenth
dix-huitième	18e	18th	eighteenth
dix-neuvième	19e	19th	nineteenth
vingtième	20e	20th	twentieth
vingt et unième	21e	21st	twenty-first
vingt-deuxième	22e	22nd	twenty-second
trentième	30e	30th	thirtieth

Quelle heure est-il ?
What time is it?

4.00 — **Il est quatre heures.**
It is four o'clock.

4.05 — **Il est quatre heures cinq.**
It is five (minutes) past four.

4.15 — **Il est quatre heures et quart.**
It is (a) quarter past four.

4.30 — **Il est quatre heures et demie.**
It is half past four. / It is four thirty.

4.45 — **Il est cinq heures moins le quart.**
It is (a) quarter to five.

4.50 — **Il est cinq heures moins dix.**
It is ten to five.

Il est midi.
It is twelve o'clock. / It is noon.

Il est minuit.
It is twelve o'clock. / It is midnight.

la date • the date

les jours days		**les mois** months	
lundi	Monday	**janvier**	January
mardi	Tuesday	**février**	February
mercredi	Wednesday	**mars**	March
jeudi	Thursday	**avril**	April
vendredi	Friday	**mai**	May
samedi	Saturday	**juin**	June
dimanche	Sunday	**juillet**	July
		août	August
		septembre	September
		octobre	October
		novembre	November
		décembre	December

Jeudi 1er mai 1994
(premier mai mille neuf cent quatre-vingt-quatorze)
Thursday, 1st May 1994

Vendredi 2 mai 1994
(deux mai mille neuf cent quatre-vingt-quatorze)
Friday, 2nd May 1994

Samedi 3 mai 1994
(trois mai mille neuf cent quatre-vingt-quatorze)
Saturday, 3rd May 1994

Dimanche 4 mai 1994
(quatre mai mille neuf cent quatre-vingt-quatorze)
Sunday, 4th May 1994

Table of phonetic symbols

Pronunciation of French

Vowels	Consonants
[i] vite, lycée	[p] pain, absolu
[e] été, donner	[b] beau, abeille
[ɛ] elle, mais	[t] table, botte
	[d] donner, sud
[a] chat, facile	[k] carré, kilo, qui
[ɑ] pas, âgé	[g] gare, second
[ɔ] donne, fort	[f] feu, phrase
[o] dos, chaud, peau	[v] voir, wagon
	[s] sonner, cerise
[u] tout, cour	[z] cousin, zéro
[y] cru, sûr	[ʃ] chose, cacher
[ø] feu, nœud	[ʒ] genou, jeter
[œ] œuf, jeune	[l] lait, facile
[ə] le, devoir	[ʀ] rare, rhume
	[m] mon, flamme
[ɛ̃] vin, plein, faim	[n] note, panne
[ɑ̃] enfant, temps	[ɲ] campagne
[ɔ̃] monter, nombre	[ŋ] camping
[œ̃] lundi, parfum	['] honte

Semi-consonants

[j] piano, voyage
[w] ouest, nouer
[ɥ] nuit

Index

Abbreviations

adj	adjective
adv.	adverb
f.	feminine
interj.	interjection
inv.	invariable
m.	masculine
n.	noun
pl.	plural
v.	verb

French – English

A

abeille [abɛj] **n. f.** : bee 63
à bientôt! [abjɛ̃to] **interj.** : see you soon ! 8, 22
s'**abriter** [sabrite] **v.** : shelter 67
accrocher [akrɔʃe] **v.** : hang* up 67
acheter [aʃte] **v.** : buy* 9, 21, 52
acteur, trice [aktœr, tris] **n.** : actor, tress 80
addition [adisjɔ̃] **n. f.** : addition 28
admirer [admire] **v.** : admire 90
aéroport [aerɔpɔr] **n. m.** : airport 72
affamé, ée [afame] **adj.** : starving 77
agent de police [aʒɑ̃dpɔlis] **m.** : policeman 18
agité, ée [aʒite] **adj.** : hectic 66
aide [ɛd] **n. f.** : help 26
aider [ede] **v.** : help 28, 87
aigle [ɛgl(ə)] **n. m.** : eagle 60, 61
aiguille [egɥij] **n. f.** : hand 31
aile [ɛl] **n. f.** : breast 90
aimer [eme] **v.** : like 57; love 8
allée [ale] **n. f.** : path 8; aisle 80
aller* [ale] **v.** : go* 20, 39, 57, 76
aller* se **coucher** [aleskuʃe] : go* to bed 75
être *allongé, ée** [ɛtralɔ̃ʒe] : be* lying down 47
ambulance [ɑ̃bylɑ̃s] **n. f.** : ambulance 49
ami, ie [ami] **n.** : friend 27
amidon [amidɔ̃] **n. m.** : starch 87
s'**amuser** [samyze] **v.** : have* fun 27, 42, 75
ananas [anana(s)] **n. m.** : pineapple 53
ancre [ɑ̃kr(ə)] **n. f.** : anchor 65
animal pl. -maux [animal, -mo] **n. m.** : animal 68, 69, 76
anniversaire [anivɛrsɛr] **n. m.** : birthday 92
anorak [anɔrak] **n. m.** : anorak 87
appareil photo [aparɛjfɔtɔ] **m.** : camera 91
apparences [aparɑ̃s] **n. f. pl.** : appearances n. pl. 27
appartement [apartəmɑ̃] **n. m.** : flat 93
applaudir [aplodir] **v.** : clap 78
apprendre* [aprɑ̃dr(ə)] **v.** : learn* 27, 30
aquarium [akwarjɔm] **n. m.** : fish bowl 11
arbitre [arbitr(ə)] **n. m.** : umpire 86
arbre [arbr(ə)] **n. m.** : tree 8, 60, 90
argent [arʒɑ̃] **n. m.** : money 21
argent de poche [arʒɑ̃dpɔʃ] **m.** : pocket money 28
armoire [armwar] **n. f.** : wardrobe 12
arrêt de bus [arɛd(ə)bys] **m.** : bus stop 23
arrivée [arive] **n. f.** : arrival 72; finish 84
arroser [aroze] **v.** : water 8
arrosoir [arozwar] **n. m.** : watering can 8
artiste [artist(ə)] **n.** : artist 77; performer 93
aspect physique [aspɛfizik] **m.** : appearance 36
assiette [asjɛt] **n. f.** : plate 14, 54
être *assis, se** [ɛtrasi, siz] : be* sitting down 11
athlète [atlɛt] **n.** : athlete 84
attendre* [atɑ̃dr(ə)] **v.** : wait (for) 23, 60, 62, 69, 92
atterrir [aterir] **v.** : land 72
attraper [atrape] **v.** : catch* 76
augmentation [ɔgmɑ̃tasjɔ̃] **n. f.** : raise 28

aujourd'hui [oʒurdɥi] **adv.** : today 27, 60, 72
au revoir! [ɔrvwar] **interj.** : bye ! 8, 14
au secours! [ɔskur] **interj.** : help ! 72
aussi [osi] **adv.** : too 75
autobus [ɔtɔbys] **n. m.** : bus 23
automne [otɔn] **n. m.** : autumn 60
autre [otr(ə)] **adj.** : other 76
autruche [otryʃ] **n. f.** : ostrich 76
avion [avjɔ̃] **n. m.** : (aero)plane 66, 72
avoir* faim [awarfɛ̃] : be* hungry 54
avoir* mal à la tête [avwarmalalatɛt] : have* a headache 49
avoir* peur [avwarpœr] : be* afraid 10, 69
avoir* soif [avwarswaf] : be* thirsty 54, 81

B

baby-sitter [ba(e)bisitœr] **n. f.** : babysitter 37
bagages [bagaʒ] **n. m. pl.** : luggage 22
bague [bag] **n. f.** : ring 43
baignoire [bɛɲwar] **n. f.** : bath 15
bâiller [baje] **v.** : yawn 13
prendre* un **bain** [prɑ̃drœ̃bɛ̃] : have* a bath 15
bal [bal] **n. m.** : dance 39
balançoire [balɑ̃swar] **n. f.** : swing 81
balcon [balkɔ̃] **n. m.** : balcony 9
balle [bal] **n. f.** : ball 86
ballon [balɔ̃] **n. m.** : ball 75, 85
banane [banan] **n. f.** : banana 53
banc [bɑ̃] **n. m.** : bench 81
barbe [barb(ə)] **n. f.** : beard 37
baromètre [barɔmɛtr(ə)] **n. m.** : barometer 67
barrette [barɛt] **n. f.** : slide 37
bateau [bato] **n. m.** : boat 65
batterie [batri] **n. f.** : drums n. pl. 79
beau, bel, belle [bo, bɛl] **adj.** : beautiful 62, 93; lovely 9, 31, 53
beaucoup (de) [boku(də)] a lot (of) 41, 56, 86
bébé [bebe] **n. m.** : baby 35, 48
avoir* **besoin** [avwarbəzwɛ̃] : need 36
beurre [bœr] **n. m.** : butter 55
bien [bjɛ̃] **adv.** : well 34, 77, 86
bientôt [bjɛ̃to] **adv.** : soon 12
bijoux [biʒu] **n. m. pl.** : jewellery 43
bille [bij] **n. f.** : marble 27
billet [bijɛ] **n. m.** : bank note 21
bizarre [bizar] **adj.** : strange 42
blanc, blanche [blɑ̃, blɑ̃ʃ] **adj.** : white 29
bleu, bleue [blø] **adj.** : blue 29
blond, onde [blɔ̃, ɔ̃d] **adj.** : blond, blonde 37
boire* [bwar] **v.** : drink* 55
bois [bwa] **n. m.** : wood 74
bon, bonne [bɔ̃, bɔn] **adj.** : good 29, 79
bonbon [bɔ̃bɔ̃] **n. m.** : sweet 28, 92
bonhomme de neige pl. bonshommes [bɔnɔmdənɛʒ, bɔ̃zɔm] **m.** : snowman 87
bon marché [bɔ̃marʃe] **adj. inv.** : cheap 21
bonnet [bɔnɛ] **n. m.** : cap 41; ski hat 87
bonnet de nuit [bɔnednɥi] **m.** : nightcap 13

botte [bɔt] **n. f.** : boot 42
bottine [bɔtin] **n. f.** : ankle boot 42
bouche [buʃ] **n. f.** : mouth 48
boucher [buʃe] **n. m.** : butcher 20
boucherie [buʃri] **n. f.** : butcher's shop 20
boucle d'oreille [bukl(ə)dɔrɛj] **f.** : earring 43
bouée [bue] **n. f.** : rubber ring 73
bougie [buʒi] **n. f.** : candle 92
boulanger, ère [bulɑ̃ʒe, ɛr] **n.** : baker 20
boulangerie [bulɑ̃ʒri] **n. f.** : bakery 20
boule [bul] **n. f.** : ball 90
boule de neige [buldənɛʒ] **f.** : snowball 87
bouquet [bukɛ] **n. m.** : bouquet 63
bouteille [butɛj] **n. f.** : bottle 56
boutique [butik] **n. f.** : shop 20
bracelet [braslɛ] **n. m.** : bracelet 43
branche [brɑ̃ʃ] **n. f.** : branch 60
bras [bra] **n. m.** : arm 35, 47
briller [brije] **v.** : shine* 66, 73; glitter 43
broche [brɔʃ] **n. f.** : brooch 43
bronzé, ée [brɔ̃ze] **adj.** : sun-tanned 73
brosse à dents [brɔsadɑ̃] **f.** : toothbrush 15
se **brosser les dents** [s(ə)brɔseledɑ̃] : brush one's teeth 15
brouillard [brujar] **n. m.** : fog 62
brun, une [brœ̃, yn] **adj.** : dark 37
bûche [byʃ] **n. f.** : log 90
bureau [byro] **n. m.** : desk 26

C

cabine téléphonique [kabintelefɔnik] **f.** : telephone kiosk 19
cadeau [kado] **n. m.** : present 90, 92
café [kafe] **n. m.** : coffee 55
cafetière [kaftjɛr] **n. f.** : coffee-pot 55
cage [kaʒ] **n. f.** : cage 93
cahier [kaje] **n. m.** : exercise book 28
caillou [kaju] **n. m.** : pebble 64
caisse [kɛs] **n. f.** : cash register 21
caissier, ière [kesje, jɛr] **n.** : cashier 21
calcul [kalkyl] **n. m.** : arithmetic 28
camion [kamjɔ̃] **n. m.** : lorry 23
campagne [kɑ̃paɲ] **n. f.** : country(side) 62
camping [kɑ̃piɲ] **n. m.** : camping 74
faire* du **camping** [fɛrdykɑ̃piɲ] : camp 74
camping-car [kɑ̃piɲkar] **n. m.** : camping car 74
canard [kanar] **n. m.** : duck 68
canne à pêche [kanapɛʃ] **f.** : fishing rod 64
canoë [kanɔe] **n. m.** : canoe 64
captiver [kaptive] **v.** : enthrall 80
caravane [karavan] **n. f.** : caravan 74
carotte [karɔt] **n. f.** : carrot 52
carré [kare] **n. m.** : square 30
carrefour [karfur] **n. m.** : crossroads n. pl. 18
cartable [kartabl(ə)] **n. m.** : satchel 28
casquette [kaskɛt] **n. f.** : cap 40
casser [kase] **v.** : break* 14

casserole [kasʀɔl] **n. f.** : saucepan **14**
ceinture [sɛ̃tyʀ] **n. f.** : belt **41**
célèbre [selebʀ(ə)] **adj.** : famous **38**
cercle [sɛʀkl(ə)] **n. m.** : circle **30**
céréales [seʀeal] **n. f. pl.** : cereal **55**
cerf [sɛʀ] **n. m.** : stag **76**
cerf-volant [sɛʀvɔlɑ̃] **n. m.** : kite **66, 91**
cerise [s(ə)ʀiz] **n. f.** : cherry **53**
chaîne stéréo [ʃɛnsteʀeo] **f.** : stereo **11**
chaise [ʃɛz] **n. f.** : chair **54**
chalet [ʃalɛ] **n. m.** : chalet **61**
chambre [ʃɑ̃bʀ(ə)] **n. f.** : bedroom **12**
chameau [ʃamo] **n. m.** : camel **76**
chamois [ʃamwa] **n. m.** : chamois **61**
champignon [ʃɑ̃piɲɔ̃] **n. m.** : mushroom **60**
champion, onne [ʃɑ̃pjɔ̃, ɔn] **n.** : champion **84**
chance [ʃɑ̃s] **n. f.** : luck **31**
changer [ʃɑ̃ʒe] **v.** : change **79**
se changer [s(ə)ʃɑ̃ʒe] **v.** : get* changed **92**
chanter faux [ʃɑ̃tefo] : sing* out of tune **79**
chanteur, euse [ʃɑ̃tœʀ, øz] **n.** : singer **79**
chapeau [ʃapo] **n. m.** : hat **40, 80**
chasser [ʃase] **v.** : hunt **38**
chat, chatte [ʃa, ʃat] **n.** : cat **68**
châtaigne [ʃatɛɲ] **n. f.** : chestnut **60**
château de sable [ʃatodsabl(ə)] **m.** : sand
    castle **73**
chaussette [ʃosɛt] **n. f.** : sock **41**
chausson [ʃosɔ̃] **n. m.** : slipper **41**
chaussure [ʃosyʀ] **n. f.** : shoe **42, 67**
chef [ʃɛf] **n. m.** : chief **38**
chef-d'œuvre [ʃɛdœvʀ(ə)] **n. m.** : masterpiece **77**
chef d'orchestre [ʃɛfdɔʀkɛstʀ(ə)] **m.** :
    conductor **78**
chemin [ʃ(ə)mɛ̃] **n. m.** : track **61**
cheminée [ʃ(ə)mine] **n. f.** : chimney **9**;
    fireplace **90**
chemise [ʃ(ə)miz] **n. f.** : shirt **41**
chemisier [ʃ(ə)mizje] **n. m.** : blouse **39**
cher, ère [ʃɛʀ] **adj.** : expensive **21, 77**
chercher [ʃɛʀʃe] **v.** : look for **93**
aller* chercher [aleʃɛʀʃe] : pick up **37**
cheval pl. -vaux [ʃ(ə)val, -vo] **n. m.** : horse **68**
chevelure [ʃəvlyʀ] **n. f.** : hair **37**
cheveux [ʃ(ə)vø] **n. m. pl.** : hair **35, 48**
chèvre [ʃɛvʀ(ə)] **n. f.** : goat **62**
chevreuil [ʃəvʀœj] **n. m.** : deer **n. inv.** **61**
chien, chienne [ʃjɛ̃, ʃjɛn] **n.** : dog **68**
chiffre [ʃifʀ(ə)] **n. m.** : figure **28**
chocolat [ʃɔkɔla] **n. m.** : chocolate **92**
choisir [ʃwaziʀ] **v.** : choose* **69**
être* au chômage [ɛtʀoʃomaʒ] : be* out of
    work **36**
chou [ʃu] **n. m.** : cabbage **52**
chouette [ʃwɛt] **n. f.** : owl **66**
ciel pl. cieux, ciels [sjɛl, sjø] **n. m.** : sky **66**
cil [sil] **n. m.** : eyelash **48**
cinéma [sinema] **n. m.** : cinema **80**
circulation [siʀkylasjɔ̃] **n. f.** : traffic **19**
cirque [siʀk(ə)] **n. m.** : circus **93**
citrouille [sitʀuj] **n. f.** : pumpkin **52**
clair, claire [klɛʀ] **adj.** : light **29**
clairière [klɛʀjɛʀ] **n. f.** : clearing **60**
classe [klas] **n. f.** : class **26**
clé [kle] **n. f.** : key **9**
clôture [klotyʀ] **n. f.** : fence **62**
clown [klun] **n. m.** : clown **93**
cochon [kɔʃɔ̃] **n. m.** : pig **62, 68**
cœur [kœʀ] **n. m.** : heart **49**
collant [kɔlɑ̃] **n. m.** : tights **n. pl.** **39**
collier [kɔlje] **n. m.** : necklace **43**
comprendre* [kɔ̃pʀɑ̃dʀ(ə)] **v.** : understand* **30**
comptoir [kɔ̃twaʀ] **n. m.** : counter **21**
se concentrer [s(ə)kɔ̃sɑ̃tʀe] **v.** : concentrate **84**
concert [kɔ̃sɛʀ] **n. m.** : concert **78, 79**
concours [kɔ̃kuʀ] **n. m.** : competition **79**
conducteur, trice [kɔ̃dyktœʀ, tʀis] **n.** : driver **23**
conduire* [kɔ̃dɥiʀ] **v.** : drive* **23, 62**
confiture [kɔ̃fityʀ] **n. f.** : jam **55**
confortable [kɔ̃fɔʀtabl(ə)] **adj.** : comfortable **11**
construire* [kɔ̃stʀɥiʀ] **v.** : build* **64**

content, ente [kɔ̃tɑ̃, ɑ̃t] **adj.** : happy **30, 31, 38**;
    glad **74**
contrôleur [kɔ̃tʀolœʀ] **n. m.** : ticket collector **22**
coq [kɔk] **n. m.** : cock **68**
coquillage [kɔkijaʒ] **n. m.** : shell **73**
corps [kɔʀ] **n. m.** : body **46, 47**
costume [kɔstym] **n. m.** : suit **39, 41**
cou [ku] **n. m.** : neck **46, 69**
coucou [kuku] **n. m.** : cuckoo clock **31**
coude [kud] **n. m.** : elbow **47**
couler [kule] **v.** : flow **64**; sink* **64**
couleur [kulœʀ] **n. f.** : colour **29**
couloir [kulwaʀ] **n. m.** : hall **10**
couper [kupe] **v.** : cut* **35**
cour [kuʀ] **n. f.** : playground **27**; back **93**
courir* [kuʀiʀ] **v.** : run* **27, 69, 84**
course [kuʀs(ə)] **n. f.** : race **84**
faire* les courses [fɛʀlekuʀs] : shop **20**
court, courte [kuʀ, kuʀt(ə)] **adj.** : short **37, 40**
cousin, ine [kuzɛ̃, in] **n.** : cousin **34, 36**
couteau [kuto] **n. m.** : knife **54**
couverture [kuvɛʀtyʀ] **n. f.** : blanket **12**
cravate [kʀavat] **n. f.** : tie **39**
crayon [kʀɛjɔ̃] **n. m.** : pencil **77**
crème [kʀɛm] **n. f.** : cream **14**
crier [kʀije] **v.** : scream **80**
crocodile [kʀɔkɔdil] **n. m.** : crocodile **69**
croire* [kʀwaʀ] **v.** : believe **9**; think* **35, 43**
cube [kyb] **n. m.** : building block **75**
cuillère [kɥijɛʀ] **n. f.** : spoon **54**
cuisine [kɥizin] **n. f.** : kitchen **14, 57**
faire* la cuisine [fɛʀlakɥizin] : cook **14**
cuisinière [kɥizinjɛʀ] **n. f.** : cooker **14**
cuisse [kɥis] **n. f.** : leg **56, 90**

D

d'abord [dabɔʀ] **adv.** : first of all **92**
d'accord ! [dakɔʀ] **interj.** : okay ! **92**
dame [dam] **n. f.** : lady **23, 46**; woman **22**
damier [damje] **n. m.** : draught-board **75**
dangereux, euse [dɑ̃ʒʀø, øz] **adj.** : dangerous
    62, 85
danser [dɑ̃se] **v.** : dance **79**
être* debout [ɛtʀədəbu] : be* standing up **47**
décider [deside] **v.** : decide **68**
décoller [dekɔle] **v.** : take* off **72**
se défendre* [s(ə)defɑ̃dʀ(ə)] **v.** : fight* back **80**
défiler [defile] **v.** : parade **93**
déjeuner [deʒœne] **n. m.** : lunch **56**
délicieux, ieuse [delisjø, jøz] **adj.** : delicious
    56, 60
demain [d(ə)mɛ̃] **adv.** : tomorrow **31, 52**
demander son chemin [dəmɑ̃desɔ̃ʃmɛ̃] : ask
    for directions **18**
demi-heure [d(ə)mijœʀ] **n. f.** : half an hour **35**
dent [dɑ̃] **n. f.** : tooth **15, 48**
dentifrice [dɑ̃tifʀis] **n. m.** : toothpaste **15**
départ [depaʀ] **n. m.** : departure **72**
se dépêcher [s(ə)depeʃe] **v.** : hurry **93**
être* désolé, ée [ɛtʀədezɔle] : be* sorry **38**
désordre [dezɔʀdʀ(ə)] **n. m.** : mess **34**
deuxième [døzjɛm] **adj.** : second **93**
devoirs [dəvwaʀ] **n. m. pl.** : homework **28**
dinde [dɛ̃d] **n. f.** : turkey **90**
dîner [dine] **n. m.** : dinner **57**
diplôme [diplom] **n. m.** : diploma **47**
dire* [diʀ] **v.** : say* **42**; tell* **52**
directeur, trice [diʀɛktœʀ, tʀis] **n.** :
    headmaster **n. m.** **26**
direction [diʀɛksjɔ̃] **n. f.** : direction **23**
disque [disk(ə)] **n. m.** : record **37**
division [divizjɔ̃] **n. f.** : division **28**
doigt [dwa] **n. m.** : finger **47**
doigt de pied [dwadpje] **m.** : toe **47**
dollar [dɔlaʀ] **n. m.** : dollar **28, 47**
domino [dɔmino] **n. m.** : domino **75**
dompteur, euse [dɔ̃tœʀ, øz] **n.** : tamer **93**
donner [dɔne] **v.** : give* **92**

dormir* [dɔʀmiʀ] **v.** : sleep* **13, 74**
dos [do] **n. m.** : back **46**
douane [dwan] **n. f.** : customs **n. pl.** **72**
douanier, ière [dwanje, jɛʀ] **n.** : customs
    officer **72**
drap [dʀa] **n. m.** : sheet **12**
dynamite [dinamit] **n. f.** : dynamite **19**

E

eau [o] **n. f.** : water **57**
éclair [eklɛʀ] **n. m.** : lightning **67**
école [ekɔl] **n. f.** : school **25, 26, 27, 30**
écouter [ekute] **v.** : listen **30**
écran [ekʀɑ̃] **n. m.** : screen **80**
écrire* [ekʀiʀ] **v.** : write* **26**
écureuil [ekyʀœj] **n. m.** : squirrel **60**
écuyer, ère [ekɥije, ɛʀ] **n.** : rider **93**
édredon [edʀədɔ̃] **n. m.** : eiderdown **13**
électrique [elɛktʀik] **adj.** : electric **79**
élégant, ante [elegɑ̃, ɑ̃t] **adj.** : smart **39**
éléphant [elefɑ̃] **n. m.** : elephant **69**
élève [elɛv] **n.** : pupil **26**
embouteillage [ɑ̃butejaʒ] **n. m.** : traffic jam **18, 19**
émeraude [emʀod] **n. f.** : emerald **43**
en colère [ɑ̃kɔlɛʀ] : angry **57**
encrier [ɑ̃kʀije] **n. m.** : inkwell **30**
s'endormir* [sɑ̃dɔʀmiʀ] **v.** : fall* asleep **62**
énerver [enɛʀve] **v.** : drive* mad **11**
enfant [ɑ̃fɑ̃] **n.** : child **27, 35**
enfin [ɑ̃fɛ̃] **adv.** : at last **30, 62**
engrais [ɑ̃gʀɛ] **n. m.** : fertilizer **52**
épaule [epol] **n. f.** : shoulder **46**
épicerie [episʀi] **n. f.** : grocer's shop **20**
éponge [epɔ̃ʒ] **n. f.** : sponge **14**
équipement [ekipmɑ̃] **n. m.** : sportsgear **85**
faire* une erreur [fɛʀynɛʀœʀ] : make* a
    mistake **28**
escalier [ɛskalje] **n. m.** : stairs **n. pl.** **10**
escarpin [ɛskaʀpɛ̃] **n. m.** : court shoe **42**
espérer [ɛspeʀe] **v.** : hope **29**
essayer* [eseje] **v.** : try* **65**
étage [etaʒ] **n. m.** : floor **93**
étagère [etaʒɛʀ] **n. f.** : shelf **14**
été [ete] **n. m.** : summer **73**
étoile [etwal] **n. f.** : star **66**
étonnant, ante [etɔnɑ̃, ɑ̃t] **adj.** : amazing **69**
être* [ɛtʀ(ə)] **v.** : be* **21, 35, 85**
être* au chômage [ɛtʀoʃomaʒ] : be* out of
    work **36**
être* en retard [ɛtʀɑ̃ʀtaʀ] : be* late **22**
étroit, oite [etʀwa, wat] **adj.** : narrow **10**
évier [evje] **n. m.** : sink **14**
excellent, ente [ɛksɛlɑ̃, ɑ̃t] **adj.** : excellent **26**
explication [ɛksplikasjɔ̃] **n. f.** : explanation **65**
expliquer [ɛksplike] **v.** : explain **63**

F

facteur [faktœʀ] **n. m.** : postman **18**
avoir* faim [awaʀfɛ̃] : be* hungry **54**
faire* la cuisine [fɛʀlakɥizin] : cook **14**
faire* la vaisselle [fɛʀlavesɛl] : do* the
    dishes **14**
faire* le ménage [fɛʀləmenaʒ] : clean up **34**
faire* les courses [fɛʀlekuʀs] : shop **20**
famille [famij] **n. f.** : family **34**
fané, ée [fane] **adj.** : wilted **63**
farce [faʀs] **n. f.** : stuffing **20**
farcir [faʀsiʀ] **v.** : stuff **20**
fatigué, ée [fatige] **adj.** : tired **13**
fauteuil [fotœj] **n. m.** : armchair **11**; seat **80**
femme [fam] **n. f.** : woman **35, 72**; wife **34**
fenêtre [fənɛtʀ(ə)] **n. f.** : window **9**
ferme [fɛʀm(ə)] **n. f.** : farm **68**
fermé, ée [fɛʀme] **adj.** : closed **9, 20, 30**

fermer [fɛʀme] **v.** : close* **84**
fermier, ière [fɛʀmje, jɛʀ] **n.** : farmer **68**
fesses [fɛs] **n. f. pl.** : bottom **46**
fête [fɛt] **n. f.** : holiday **89**
feu [fø] **n. m.** : fire **74**
feu (de signalisation) [fø(dəsiɲalizasjɔ̃)] **n. m.** : (traffic) light **18**
feuille [fœj] **n. f.** : leaf **60**
fidèle [fidɛl] **adj.** : faithful **68**
filet [filɛ] **n. m.** : net **86**
filet à papillons [fileapapijɔ̃] **m.** : butterfly net **85**
fille [fij] **n. f.** : girl **23, 35, 37, 39**; daughter **34**
film [film] **n. m.** : film **80**
fils [fis] **n. m.** : son **34**
fin [fɛ̃] **n. f.** : end **93**
flaque [flak] **n. f.** : puddle **67**
fleur [flœʀ] **n. f.** : flower **8, 63**
fleuriste [flœʀist(ə)] **n.** : florist **63**
flûte [flyt] **n. f.** : flute **78**
foncé, ée [fɔ̃se] **adj.** : dark **29**
fontaine [fɔ̃tɛn] **n. f.** : fountain **81**
forêt [fɔʀɛ] **n. f.** : forest **60**
forme [fɔʀm(ə)] **n. f.** : shape **30**
fort, forte [fɔʀ, fɔʀt(ə)] **adj.** : strong **36, 85**
four [fuʀ] **n. m.** : oven **14**
fourchette [fuʀʃɛt] **n. f.** : fork **54**
fourmi [fuʀmi] **n. f.** : ant **91**
fraise [fʀɛz] **n. f.** : strawberry **53**
frange [fʀɑ̃ʒ] **n. f.** : fringe **37**
froid, froide [fʀwa, fʀwad] **adj.** : cold **74, 87, 91**
fromage [fʀɔmaʒ] **n. m.** : cheese **56**
froncer les sourcils [fʀɔ̃selesuʀsi] : frown **46**
front [fʀɔ̃] **n. m.** : forehead **48**
fruits [fʀɥi] **n. m. pl.** : fruit **53**
fumée [fyme] **n. f.** : smoke **74**

G

gagner [gaɲe] **v.** : win* **84, 86**
gai, gaie [ge] **adj.** : happy **15**
garage [gaʀaʒ] **n. m.** : garage **9**
garçon [gaʀsɔ̃] **n. m.** : boy **35**
garder [gaʀde] **v.** : guard **68**
gare [gaʀ] **n. f.** : station **22**
gâteau [gato] **n. m.** : cake **14, 92**
gazon [gazɔ̃] **n. m.** : lawn **8**
genou [ʒ(ə)nu] **n. m.** : knee **47**
gens [ʒɑ̃] **n. m. pl.** : people **33**
gentil, ille [ʒɑ̃ti, ij] **adj.** : nice **38**
girafe [ʒiʀaf] **n. f.** : giraffe **69, 76**
girouette [ʒiʀwɛt] **n. f.** : weathercock **68**
glace [glas] **n. f.** : ice cream **92**
glisser [glise] **v.** : slide* **81**
gomme [gɔm] **n. f.** : rubber **77**
goûter d'anniversaire [gutedaniveʀsɛʀ] **m.** : birthday party **92**
grand, grande [gʀɑ̃, gʀɑ̃d] **adj.** : tall **36**; big **42**
grand-mère [gʀɑ̃mɛʀ] **n. f.** : grandmother **34**
grand-père [gʀɑ̃pɛʀ] **n. m.** : grandfather **34**
faire* **griller** [fɛʀgʀije] : grill **74**
gris, grise [gʀi, gʀiz] **adj.** : grey **29**
gros, grosse [gʀo, gʀos] **adj.** : fat **36**
guirlande [giʀlɑ̃d] **n. f.** : garland **90**
guitare [gitaʀ] **n. f.** : guitar **74, 79**
gymnase [ʒimnaz] **n. m.** : gym **85**
gymnastique [ʒimnastik] **n. f.** : gymnastics **n. pl. 85**

H

s'**habiller** [sabije] **v.** : get* dressed **40**
habiter [abite] **v.** : live **9**
haie [ɛ] **n. f.** : hedge **8**
haltères [altɛʀ] **n. m. pl.** : weights **85**
hangar [ɑ̃gaʀ] **n. m.** : hangar **72**
haricot vert [ˈaʀikovɛʀ] **m.** : green bean **52**

harpe [ˈaʀp(ə)] **n. f.** : harp **79**
herbe [ɛʀb(ə)] **n. f.** : grass **60**
héros [ˈeʀo] **n. m.** : hero **80**
heure [œʀ] **n. f.** : hour **31, 35**; time **14, 31**
heureux, euse [œʀø, øz] **adj.** : happy **35**
hippopotame [ipɔpɔtam] **n. m.** : hippopotamus **69**
hiver [ivɛʀ] **n. m.** : winter **87**
homme [ɔm] **n. m.** : man **35**
hôpital pl. **-taux** [ɔpital, -to] **n. m.** : hospital **49**
horloge [ɔʀlɔʒ] **n. f.** : clock **22**
hôtesse de l'air [otesdəlɛʀ] **f.** : air hostess **72**
humain, aine [ymɛ̃, ɛn] **adj.** : human **47**

I

idée [ide] **n. f.** : idea **66, 68**
immeuble [im(m)œbl(ə)] **n. m.** : building **18**
imperméable [ɛ̃pɛʀmeabl(ə)] **n. m.** : raincoat **40, 67**
impossible [ɛ̃pɔsibl(ə)] **adj.** : impossible **9**
Indien, ienne [ɛ̃djɛ̃, jɛn] **n.** : Indian **64**
indien, ienne [ɛ̃djɛ̃, jɛn] **adj.** : Indian **38**
indiquer [ɛ̃dike] **v.** : show* **31**
infirmière [ɛ̃fiʀmjɛʀ] **n. f.** : nurse **49**
influence [ɛ̃flyɑ̃s] **n. f.** : influence **26**
inquiet, ète [ɛ̃kjɛ, ɛt] **adj.** : worried **49**
instrument [ɛ̃stʀymɑ̃] **n. m.** : instrument **79**
interdit, ite [ɛ̃teʀdi, it] **adj.** : forbidden **18**
invitation [ɛ̃vitasjɔ̃] **n. f.** : invitation **92**
invité, ée [ɛ̃vite] **n.** : guest **40, 92**
inviter [ɛ̃vite] **v.** : invite **38**

J

jambe [ʒɑ̃b] **n. f.** : leg **47**
jardin [ʒaʀdɛ̃] **n. m.** : garden **8, 69**
jaune [ʒon] **adj.** : yellow **29**
jean [dʒin] **n. m.** : jeans **n. pl. 40**
jetée [ʒ(ə)te] **n. f.** : jetty **65**
jeu [ʒø] **n. m.** : game **75**
jeu d'échecs [ʒødeʃɛk] **m.** : chess **75**
jeu de dames [ʒød(ə)dam] **m.** : checkers **n. pl. 75**
jeune [ʒœn] **adj.** : young **35**
jogging [dʒɔgiɲ] **n. m.** : tracksuit **85**
joli, ie [ʒɔli] **adj.** : lovely **39**
jongleur, euse [ʒɔ̃glœʀ, øz] **n.** : juggler **93**
joue [ʒu] **n. f.** : cheek **48**
jouer [ʒwe] **v.** : play **27, 75, 78, 85, 86**
jouet [ʒwe] **n. m.** : toy **75**
joueur, euse [ʒwœʀ, øz] **n.** : player **86**
jour [ʒuʀ] **n. m.** : day **68**
jupe [ʒyp] **n. f.** : skirt **40**
jupon [ʒypɔ̃] **n. m.** : petticoat **39**
jus [ʒy] **n. m.** : juice **92**

K

kangourou [kɑ̃guʀu] **n. m.** : kangaroo **76**
kilo [kilo] **n. m.** : kilo **20**
klaxonner [klaksɔne] **v.** : hoot **19**

L

lacet [lasɛ] **n. m.** : shoelace **42**
laid, laide [lɛ, lɛd] **adj.** : ugly **36**
laisser [lese] **v.** : let* **13**; leave* **54**
lait [lɛ] **n. m.** : milk **21, 55**
lampe [lɑ̃p] **n. f.** : lamp **12**
lancer* [lɑ̃se] **v.** : throw* **87**
langue [lɑ̃g] **n. f.** : tongue **48**
lapin [lapɛ̃] **n. m.** : rabbit **62**

large [laʀʒ(ə)] **adj.** : big **40**
lavabo [lavabo] **n. m.** : hand basin **15**
se **laver** [s(ə)lave] **v.** : wash oneself **15**
légumes [legym] **n. m. pl.** : vegetables **n. pl. 52**
se **lever** [s(ə)l(ə)ve] **v.** : get* up **12**
limonade [limɔnad] **n. f.** : lemonade **92**
lion, lionne [ljɔ̃, ljɔn] **n.** : lion **69**
lire* [liʀ] **v.** : read* **11**
lit [li] **n. m.** : bed **13**
livre [livʀ(ə)] **n. m.** : book **11, 27, 30**
locomotive [lɔkɔmɔtiv] **n. f.** : engine **22**
loisirs [lwaziʀ] **n. m. pl.** : leisure **71**
long, longue [lɔ̃, lɔ̃g] **adj.** : long **37, 69**
louche [luʃ] **n. f.** : ladle **57**
louer [lwe] **v.** : rent **9, 93**
lourd, lourde [luʀ, luʀd(ə)] **adj.** : heavy **22**
luge [lyʒ] **n. f.** : sleigh **87**
lumière [lymjɛʀ] **n. f.** : light **10**
lune [lyn] **n. f.** : moon **66**
lunettes [lynɛt] **n. f. pl.** : glasses **n. pl. 46**
lunettes de soleil [lynɛtdəsɔlɛj] **f. pl.** : sunglasses **n. pl. 73**

M

magasin [magazɛ̃] **n. m.** : shop **20**
magique [maʒik] **adj.** : magic **52**
maigre [mɛgʀ(ə)] **adj.** : thin **36**
maillot [majo] **n. m.** : vest **40**
maillot de bain [majodbɛ̃] **m.** : bathing suit **73**
main [mɛ̃] **n. f.** : hand **47**
maintenant [mɛ̃tnɑ̃] **adv.** : now **66, 72, 92**
maison [mɛzɔ̃] **n. f.** : house **7, 9, 10, 67, 68**
maître, maîtresse [mɛtʀ(ə), mɛtʀɛs] **n.** : schoolteacher **26**
malade [malad] **adj.** : sick **49**
avoir* **mal à la tête** [avwaʀmalalatɛt] : have* a headache **49**
maman [mamɑ̃] **n. f.** : mother **35**
manger [mɑ̃ʒe] **v.** : eat* **54, 56, 60, 77, 92**
manteau [mɑ̃to] **n. m.** : coat **40**
mappemonde [mapmɔ̃d] **n. f.** : globe **30**
marche [maʀʃ(ə)] **n. f.** : step **10**
mare [maʀ] **n. f.** : pond **68**
marguerite [maʀgəʀit] **n. f.** : daisy **63**
mari [maʀi] **n. m.** : husband **34**
marron [maʀɔ̃] **adj. inv.** : brown **29**
masseur, euse [masœʀ, øz] **n.** : masseur, euse **47**
match [matʃ] **n. m.** : game **86**
matelas [matla] **n. m.** : mattress **12**
matin [matɛ̃] **n. m.** : morning **52, 62**
médaille [medaj] **n. f.** : medal **84**
médecin [medsɛ̃] **n. m.** : doctor **49**
médicament [medikamɑ̃] **n. m.** : medicine **14, 49**
meilleur, eure [mejœʀ] **adj.** : best **29**
faire* **le ménage** [fɛʀləmenaʒ] : clean up **34**
menton [mɑ̃tɔ̃] **n. m.** : chin **48**
mer [mɛʀ] **n. f.** : sea **65**
merci ! [mɛʀsi] **interj.** : thanks ! **28, 36**
mère [mɛʀ] **n. f.** : mother **34**
micro [mikʀo] **n. m.** : microphone **79**
miel [mjɛl] **n. m.** : honey **55**
mieux [mjø] **adv.** : better **72**
mignon, onne [miɲɔ̃, ɔn] **adj.** : cute **48**
minute [minyt] **n. f.** : minute **31**
miroir [miʀwaʀ] **n. m.** : mirror **15**
mite [mit] **n. f.** : moth **41**
mobile [mɔbil] **n. m.** : mobile **75**
mois [mwa] **n. m.** : month **93**
monnaie [mɔnɛ] **n. f.** : change **21**
monsieur pl. **messieurs** [məsjø, mesjø] **n. m.** : gentleman **23**
montagne [mɔ̃taɲ] **n. f.** : mountain **61**
monter à cheval [mɔ̃teaʃval] : ride* a horse **68**
montre [mɔ̃tʀ(ə)] **n. f.** : watch **31, 48**
montrer [mɔ̃tʀe] **v.** : show* **72**
montrer le chemin [mɔ̃tʀelʃəmɛ̃] : show* the way **18**
moto [mɔto] **n. f.** : motorcycle **23**

mouette [mwɛt] n. f. : seagull 66
mouillé, ée [muje] **adj.** : wet 67
mourir* [muʀiʀ] v. : die* 49
moustache [mustaʃ] n. f. : moustache 37
moyens de transport [mwajɛ̃dtʀɑ̃spɔʀ] m. pl : transport 23
multiplication [myltiplikasjɔ̃] n. f. : multiplication 28
mur [myʀ] n. m. : wall 9
mûr, mûre [myʀ] **adj.** : ripe 53
musclé, ée [myskle] **adj.** : muscled 47
musée [myze] n. m. : museum 61
musicien, ienne [myzisjɛ̃, jɛn] n. : musician 79
musique [myzik] n. f. : music 78, 79

N

nager* [naʒe] v. : swim* 65, 68
nappe [nap] n. f. : tablecloth 56
nature [natyʀ] n. f. : nature 59
navire [naviʀ] n. m. : ship 65
neige [nɛʒ] n. f. : snow 87
neiger [neʒe] v. : snow 87
neuf, neuve [nœf, nœv] **adj.** : new 39
neveu [n(ə)vø] n. m. : nephew 55, 92
nez [ne] n. m. : nose 48
niche [niʃ] n. f. : kennel 68
nid [ni] n. m. : nest 60
nièce [njɛs] n. f. : niece 37
Noël [nɔɛl] n. m. : Christmas 90
nœud papillon [nøpapijɔ̃] m. : bow tie 39
noir, noire [nwaʀ] **adj.** : black 29
nourriture [nuʀityʀ] n. f. : food 51
nouveau, vel, velle [nuvo, vɛl] **adj.** : new 69
nuage [nɥaʒ] n. m. : cloud 66
nuit [nɥi] n. f. : night 66

O

œil pl. yeux [œj, jø] n. m. : eye 48, 84
œillet [œjɛ] n. m. : carnation 63
œuf [œf] n. m. : egg 55, 60, 61
oignon [ɔɲɔ̃] n. m. : onion 52
oiseau [wazo] n. m. : bird 61, 62
omelette [ɔmlɛt] n. f. : omelet 60
oncle [ɔ̃kl(ə)] n. m. : uncle 14, 34
or [ɔʀ] n. m. : gold 43
orage [ɔʀaʒ] n. m. : storm 67
orange [ɔʀɑ̃ʒ] n. f. : orange 53, 92
orange [ɔʀɑ̃ʒ] **adj. inv.** : orange 29
orchestre [ɔʀkɛstʀ(ə)] n. m. : orchestra 78
oreille [ɔʀɛj] n. f. : ear 48
oreiller [ɔʀeje] n. m. : pillow 13
os [ɔs] n. m. : bone 54
oublier [ublije] v. : forget* 22, 41, 84
ours [uʀs] n. m. : bear 30, 38
ours en peluche [uʀsɑ̃plyʃ] m. : teddy bear 75
ouvert, erte [uvɛʀ, ɛʀt(ə)] **adj.** : open 30
ouvrir* [uvʀiʀ] v. : open 84

P

page [paʒ] n. f. : page 26
pain [pɛ̃] n. m. : bread 55
palette [palɛt] n. f. : palette 77
palmier [palmje] n. m. : palm tree 73
panier [panje] n. m. : basket 91
panneau (de signalisation) [pano(dəsiɲalizasjɔ̃)] n. m. : road sign 23
pantalon [pɑ̃talɔ̃] n. m. : trousers **n. pl.** 40
papier [papje] n. m. : paper 77
papier peint [papjepɛ̃] m. : wallpaper 69
papillon [papijɔ̃] n. m. : butterfly 85
paquet [pakɛ] n. m. : parcel 19

parapluie [paʀaplɥi] n. m. : umbrella 67
parasol [paʀasɔl] n. m. : beach umbrella 73
parc [paʀk] n. m. : park 81
parier [paʀje] v. : bet* 52
parking [paʀkiŋ] n. m. : car park 18
parler [paʀle] v. : talk* 76
par terre [paʀtɛʀ] : on the ground 27
partie [paʀti] n. f. : part 47; game 75
passage pour piétons [pasaʒpuʀpjetɔ̃] m. : zebra crossing 23
passager, ère [pasaʒe, ɛʀ] n. : passenger 23
passeport [paspɔʀ] n. m. : passport 72
se passer [s(ə)pase] v. : happen 76
patin à roulettes [patɛ̃aʀulɛt] m. : roller skate 85
pauvre [povʀ(ə)] **adj.** : poor 38, 77
payer* [peje] v. : pay* 21
paysage [peizaʒ] n. m. : landscape 62
pêche [pɛʃ] n. f. : peach 53
pêcher [peʃe] v. : catch* 64
pêcheur, euse [peʃœʀ, øz] n. : fisherman n. m. 64
peigne [pɛɲ] n. m. : comb 15
peignoir [pɛɲwaʀ] n. m. : bathrobe 15
peindre* [pɛ̃dʀ(ə)] v. : paint 77
peinture [pɛ̃tyʀ] n. f. : painting 77
pelle [pɛl] n. f. : shovel 8
pelouse [pəluz] n. f. : lawn 8
penderie [pɑ̃dʀi] n. f. : wardrobe 41
penser [pɑ̃se] v. : think* 87
père [pɛʀ] n. m. : father 34
perle [pɛʀl(ə)] n. f. : bead 43
personnalité [pɛʀsɔnalite] n. f. : personality 38
peser [pəze] v. : weigh 20
pétale [petal] n. m. : petal 63
petit, ite [p(ə)ti, it] **adj.** : small 36
petit déjeuner [p(ə)tideʒœne] m. : breakfast 55
petit pois [ptipwa] m. : pea 52
avoir* **peur** [avwaʀpœʀ] : be* afraid 10, 69
peut-être [pøtɛtʀ(ə)] **adv.** : perhaps 49
phare [faʀ] n. m. : headlight 19; lighthouse 65
photo [fɔtɔ] n. f. : photo 46, 91
prendre* **une photo** [pʀɑ̃dʀynfɔtɔ] : take* a photo 46, 91
piano [pjano] n. m. : piano 78
pièce [pjɛs] n. f. : coin 21
pied [pje] n. m. : foot 42, 47
piéton, onne [pjetɔ̃, ɔn] n. : pedestrian 19
pinceau [pɛ̃so] n. m. : paint brush 77
pingouin [pɛ̃gwɛ̃] n. m. : penguin 76
pique-nique [piknik] n. m. : picnic 91
piqûre [pikyʀ] n. f. : injection 49
piste [pist(ə)] n. f. : ring 93; slope 87; track 84; runway 72
placard [plakaʀ] n. m. : cupboard 14
plage [plaʒ] n. f. : beach 73
planche à roulettes [plɑ̃ʃaʀulɛt] f. : skate board 85
plancher [plɑ̃ʃe] n. m. : floor 10
plante [plɑ̃t] n. f. : plant 52, 63
planter [plɑ̃te] v. : plant 8
plante verte [plɑ̃tvɛʀt] f. : green plant 63
plat [pla] n. m. : dish 54, 56
plein, pleine [plɛ̃, plɛn] **adj.** : full 30
pleuvoir* [pløvwaʀ] v. : rain 52
pluie [plɥi] n. f. : rain 52, 67
pneu [pnø] n. m. : tyre 19
podium [pɔdjɔm] n. m. : podium 84
poêle [pwal] n. f. : frying pan 57
poire [pwaʀ] n. f. : pear 53
poireau [pwaʀo] n. m. : leek 52
poisson [pwasɔ̃] n. m. : fish 57, 64, 76
poisson rouge [pwasɔ̃ʀuʒ] m. : goldfish 11
poivre [pwavʀ(ə)] n. m. : pepper 54
poivron [pwavʀɔ̃] n. m. : sweet pepper 52
poli, ie [pɔli] **adj.** : polite 38
police [pɔlis] n. f. : police 65
pomme [pɔm] n. f. : apple 53
pomme de terre [pɔmdətɛʀ] f. : potato 52
pont [pɔ̃] n. m. : bridge 64
port [pɔʀ] n. m. : harbour 65
porte [pɔʀt] n. f. : door 9
portefeuille [pɔʀtəfœj] n. m. : wallet 21

portemanteau [pɔʀtmɑ̃to] n. m. : peg 41; coatstand 40
porte-monnaie [pɔʀtmɔnɛ] n. m. inv. : purse 21
porter [pɔʀte] v. : hold* 35; wear* 39, 46
portrait [pɔʀtʀɛ] n. m. : portrait 77
poser [poze] v. : put* 27
poste [pɔst] n. f. : post office 18
poubelle [pubɛl] n. f. : dustbin 14
poulailler [pulaje] n. m. : henhouse 68
poule [pul] n. f. : hen 68
poulet [pulɛ] n. m. : chicken 20, 56, 91
poupée [pupe] n. f. : doll 9, 75
pousser [puse] v. : grow* 52
poussette [pusɛt] n. f. : puschair 81
pouvoir* [puvwaʀ] v. : can* 80
prairie [pʀeʀi] n. f. : meadow 62
pratique [pʀatik] **adj.** : practical 55
premier, ière [pʀəmje, jɛʀ] **adj.** : first 40, 93
prendre* **une photo** [pʀɑ̃dʀynfɔtɔ] : take* a photo 46, 91
presse-fruits [pʀɛsfʀɥi] n. m. inv. : orange squeezer 36
printemps [pʀɛ̃tɑ̃] n. m. : spring 8
prix [pʀi] n. m. : price 9
professeur [pʀɔfesœʀ] n. m. : teacher 27
profond, onde [pʀɔfɔ̃, ɔ̃d] **adj.** : deep 64
projecteur [pʀɔʒɛktœʀ] n. m. : projector 80
propre [pʀɔpʀ(ə)] **adj.** : clean 15
provoquer [pʀɔvɔke] v. : cause 19
public [pyblik] n. m. : audience 78
pull-over [pylɔvɛʀ] n. m. : pullover 41
puzzle [pœzl(ə)] n. m. : puzzle 75
pyjama [piʒama] n. m. : pyjamas **n. pl.** 13

Q

quai [ke] n. m. : platform 22
question [kɛstjɔ̃] n. f. : question 27
queue de cheval [kødʃəval] f. : ponytail 37

R

radis [ʀadi] n. m. : radish 52
raide [ʀɛd] **adj.** : straight 37
raisin [ʀɛzɛ̃] n. m. : grape 53
rampe [ʀɑ̃p] n. f. : bannisters **n. pl.** 10
raquette [ʀakɛt] n. f. : bat 86
râteau [ʀɑto] n. m. : rake 8
rayure [ʀejyʀ] n. f. : stripe 29
se réchauffer [s(ə)ʀeʃofe] v. : warm oneself 74
récréation [ʀekʀeasjɔ̃] n. f. : playtime 27
rectangle [ʀɛktɑ̃gl(ə)] n. m. : rectangle 30
réfrigérateur [ʀefʀiʒeʀatœʀ] n. m. : fridge 57
regarder la télévision [ʀəgaʀdelatelevizjɔ̃] : watch television 11
règle [ʀɛgl(ə)] n. f. : ruler 77
repas [ʀ(ə)pɑ] n. m. : meal 91
respirer [ʀɛspiʀe] v. : breathe 49
être* **en retard** [ɛtʀɑ̃ʀtaʀ] : be* late 22
réveil [ʀevɛj] n. m. : alarm clock 12, 31
réveille-matin [ʀevɛjmatɛ̃] n. m. inv. : alarm-clock 12
se réveiller [s(ə)ʀeveje] v. : wake* up 12
revenir* [ʀəvniʀ] v. : come* back 64
riche [ʀiʃ] **adj.** : rich 38
rive [ʀiv] n. f. : bank 64
rivière [ʀivjɛʀ] n. f. : river 64
riz [ʀi] n. m. : rice 56
robe [ʀɔb] n. f. : dress 39
robe de chambre [ʀɔbdəʃɑ̃bʀ(ə)] f. : dressing gown 13
robinet [ʀɔbinɛ] n. m. : tap 15
rond, ronde [ʀɔ̃, ʀɔ̃d] **adj.** : round 30
rose [ʀoz] n. f. : rose 63
rose [ʀoz] **adj.** : pink 29
rouge [ʀuʒ] **adj.** : red 29

rouler [ʀule] **v.** : roll 43
roux, rousse [ʀu, ʀus] **adj.** : red-haired 37
rubis [ʀybi] **n. m.** : ruby 43
rue [ʀy] **n. f.** : street 18, 93
ruisseau [ʀɥiso] **n. m.** : brook 62

S

sable [sɑbl(ə)] **n. m.** : sand 73
sac à dos [sakado] **m.** : rucksack 74
sac de couchage [sakdəkuʃaʒ] **m.** : sleeping bag 74
salade [salad] **n. f.** : lettuce 52
sale [sal] **adj.** : dirty 15
salle de bains [saldəbɛ̃] **f.** : bathroom 15
salle de classe [saldəklas] **f.** : classroom 26
salle de jeux [saldəʒø] **f.** : playroom 75
salle de séjour [saldəseʒuʀ] **f.** : sitting-room 11
salon [salɔ̃] **n. m.** : sitting-room 69; drawing room 93
sandale [sɑ̃dal] **n. f.** : sandal 47
sandwich [sɑ̃dwitʃ] **n. m.** : sandwich 91
santé [sɑ̃te] **n. f.** : health 49
sapin [sapɛ̃] **n. m.** : fir tree 64
sauter [sote] **v.** : jump 76, 84
sauvage [sovaʒ] **adj.** : wild 69
savoir * [savwaʀ] **v.** : know * 29, 41, 60
savon [savɔ̃] **n. m.** : soap 15
saxophone [saksɔfɔn] **n. m.** : saxophone 79
scène [sɛn] **n. f.** : stage 78
seconde [s(ə)gɔ̃d] **n. f.** : second 31
sel [sɛl] **n. m.** : salt 54
semaine [s(ə)mɛn] **n. f.** : week 28
seringue [s(ə)ʀɛ̃g] **n. f.** : syringe 49
serpent [sɛʀpɑ̃] **n. m.** : snake 69
serrure [seʀyʀ] **n. f.** : lock 9
serviette [sɛʀvjɛt] **n. f.** : towel 15; napkin 54
shampooing [ʃɑ̃pwɛ̃] **n. m.** : shampoo 15
short [ʃɔʀt] **n. m.** : shorts n. pl. 85
siècle [sjɛkl(ə)] **n. m.** : century 93
singe [sɛ̃ʒ] **n. m.** : monkey 69
ski [ski] **n. m.** : ski 87; skiing 87
skier [skje] **v.** : ski 87
faire * du **ski nautique** [fɛʀdyskinotik] : water-ski * 65
avoir * **soif** [avwaʀswaf] : be * thirsty 54, 81
soigner [swaɲe] **v.** : look after 49
ce **soir** [səswaʀ] : tonight adv. 39
sol [sɔl] **n. m.** : floor 43
soldes [sɔld(ə)] **n. m. pl.** : sale 31
soleil [sɔlɛj] **n. m.** : sun 62, 73
solide [sɔlid] **adj.** : sturdy 64
solution [sɔlysjɔ̃] **n. f.** : solution 55
sombre [sɔ̃bʀ(ə)] **adj.** : dark 10
sommet [sɔmɛ] **n. m.** : peak 61
somnambule [sɔmnɑ̃byl] **n.** : sleepwalker 57
sonner [sɔne] **v.** : ring * 12, 31
soucoupe volante [sukupvɔlɑ̃t] **f.** : flying saucer 66
souffler [sufle] **v.** : blow * 65, 92
soupe [sup] **n. f.** : soup 57
soupière [supjɛʀ] **n. f.** : soup tureen 57
sourcil [suʀsil] **n. m.** : eyebrow 48
sourire * [suʀiʀ] **v.** : smile 91
soustraction [sustʀaksjɔ̃] **n. f.** : subtraction 28
spectacle [spɛktakl(ə)] **n. m.** : performance 93
spectateur, trice [spɛktatœʀ, tʀis] **n.** : spectator 93; viewer 80
sport [spɔʀ] **n. m.** : sport 83
stade [stad] **n. m.** : stadium 84

stationner [stasjɔne] **v.** : park 18
stylo [stilɔ] **n. m.** : pen 28
sucette [sysɛt] **n. f.** : lollipop 92
sucre [sykʀ(ə)] **n. m.** : sugar 21, 55
sucrier [sykʀije] **n. m.** : sugar dispenser 55
supermarché [sypɛʀmaʀʃe] **n. m.** : supermarket 20
supporter [sypɔʀte] **v.** : stand * 42
sûr, sûre [syʀ] **adj.** : sure 20
surprise [syʀpʀiz] **n. f.** : surprise 14, 38
surveiller [syʀveje] **v.** : watch (over) 27
synthétiseur [sɛ̃tetizœʀ] **n. m.** : synthesizer 79

T

table [tabl(ə)] **n. f.** : table 54
tableau [tablo] **n. m.** : blackboard 26; painting 77, 93
table de chevet [tabldəʃvɛ] **f.** : bedside table 12
tablier [tablije] **n. m.** : smock 77
tabouret [tabuʀɛ] **n. m.** : stool 14
tache [taʃ] **n. f.** : stain 77
se **taire** * [s(ə)tɛʀ] **v.** : keep * one's mouth shut 38
talkie-walkie [tɔkiwɔlki] **n. m.** : walkie-talkie 61
talon [talɔ̃] **n. m.** : heel 42
tante [tɑ̃t] **n. f.** : aunt 34
tapis [tapi] **n. m.** : rug 12
tapisser [tapise] **v.** : paper 69
tard [taʀ] **adv.** : late 13, 29
tarte [taʀt(ə)] **n. f.** : tart 56
tasse [tɑs] **n. f.** : cup 55
taxi [taksi] **n. m.** : taxi 23
tee-shirt [tiʃœʀt] **n. m.** : tee-shirt 41
téléphone [telefɔn] **n. m.** : telephone 11
téléphoner [telefɔne] **v.** : make * a telephone call 19
télévision [televizjɔ̃] **n. f.** : television 11
temps [tɑ̃] **n. m.** : weather 67
tennis [tenis] **n. m.** : tennis shoe 42
tennis de table [tenisdətabl] **m.** : table tennis 86
tente [tɑ̃t] **n. f.** : tent 74
tête [tet] **n. f.** : head 46
thé [te] **n. m.** : tea 55
théière [tejɛʀ] **n. f.** : teapot 55
ticket de bus [tikɛdbys] **m.** : bus fare 28
tige [tiʒ] **n. f.** : stem 63
timbre [tɛ̃bʀ(ə)] **n. m.** : stamp 21
tiroir [tiʀwaʀ] **n. m.** : drawer 41
toboggan [tɔbɔgɑ̃] **n. m.** : slide 81
toile [twal] **n. f.** : canvas 77
toit [twa] **n. m.** : roof 9, 68
tomate [tɔmat] **n. f.** : tomato 91
tomber [tɔ̃be] **v.** : fall * 60, 87
tondeuse à gazon [tɔ̃døzagazɔ̃] **f.** : lawn mower 8
tonnerre [tɔnɛʀ] **n. m.** : thunder 67
torero [tɔʀeʀo] **n. m.** : bullfighter 40
torrent [tɔʀɑ̃] **n. m.** : mountain stream 61
tôt [to] **adv.** : early 62
total pl. -taux [tɔtal, -to] **n. m.** : total 28
toujours [tuʒuʀ] **adv.** : always 29
trace [tʀas] **n. f.** : track 30
train [tʀɛ̃] **n. m.** : train 22
travail pl. -vaux [tʀavaj, -vo] **n. m.** : work 52; job 29
bien **travailler** [bjɛ̃tʀavaje] : work hard 26
traverser (la rue) [tʀavɛʀse(laʀy)] **v.** : cross (the street) 18, 19
très [tʀɛ] **adv.** : very 39, 62
tresse [tʀɛs] **n. f.** : plait 37

triangle [tʀijɑ̃gl(ə)] **n. m.** : triangle 30
trompette [tʀɔ̃pɛt] **n. f.** : trumpet 78
tronc [tʀɔ̃] **n. m.** : trunk 60
trop [tʀo] **adv.** : too 40, 42, 62, 85
trottoir [tʀɔtwaʀ] **n. m.** : pavement 18
trouver [tʀuve] **v.** : find * 39, 60, 61
tube de peinture [tybdəpɛ̃tyʀ] **m.** : tube of paint 77
tulipe [tylip] **n. f.** : tulip 63

V

vacances [vakɑ̃s] **n. f. pl.** : holidays n. pl. 22, 73
vache [vaʃ] **n. f.** : cow 62
vainqueur [vɛ̃kœʀ] **n. m.** : winner 84
faire * la **vaisselle** [fɛʀlavɛsɛl] : do * the dishes 14
valise [valiz] **n. f.** : suitcase 22
vallée [vale] **n. f.** : valley 61
vase [vɑz] **n. m.** : vase 11
veau [vo] **n. m.** : calf 62
vélo [velo] **n. m.** : bicycle 18; bike 19
vendeur, euse [vɑ̃dœʀ, øz] **n.** : salesperson 21
vendre * [vɑ̃dʀ(ə)] **v.** : sell * 9, 21
vent [vɑ̃] **n. m.** : wind 65
ventre [vɑ̃tʀ(ə)] **n. m.** : stomach 46
vérifier [veʀifje] **v.** : check 20
verre [vɛʀ] **n. m.** : glass 14, 54
vert, verte [vɛʀ, vɛʀt(ə)] **adj.** : green 18, 29
veste [vɛst(ə)] **n. f.** : jacket 39, 40
vêtements [vɛtmɑ̃] **n. m. pl.** : clothes n. pl. 39, 40, 41
viande [vjɑ̃d] **n. f.** : meat 56, 74
vide [vid] **adj.** : empty 30
vider [vide] **v.** : empty 57
vieux, vieil, vieille [vjø, vjɛj] **adj.** : old 36
ville [vil] **n. f.** : town 17, 29
violet, ette [vjɔlɛ, ɛt] **adj.** : purple 29
violon [vjɔlɔ̃] **n. m.** : violin 78
visage [vizaʒ] **n. m.** : face 48
vite [vit] **adv.** : quickly 69
voie [vwa] **n. f.** : track 22
voile [vwal] **n. f.** : sail 65
voir * [vwaʀ] **v.** : see * 34, 46, 52, 53, 56, 67, 76, 80
voiture [vwatyʀ] **n. f.** : car 18, 19
voler [vɔle] **v.** : fly * 62
volet [vɔlɛ] **n. m.** : shutter 9
vouloir * [vulwaʀ] **v.** : want 20, 29, 53
vrai, vraie [vʀɛ] **adj.** : real 57, 64
vraiment [vʀɛmɑ̃] **adv.** : really 55, 77

W

wagon [vagɔ̃] **n. m.** : carriage 22

Y

yaourt [jauʀt] **n. m.** : yogurt 56

Z

zèbre [zɛbʀ(ə)] **n. m.** : zebra 69, 76
zoo [zoo] **n. m.** : zoo 76

English – French

A

actor, tress ['æktə', tris] n. : acteur, trice **80**
addition [ə'diʃ(ə)n] n. : addition n. f. **28**
admire [əd'maiə'] v. : admirer **90**
aeroplane ['εərəplein] n. : avion n. m. **66, 72**
be* afraid [bi:ə'freid] : avoir* peur **10, 69**
air hostess [εə'houstis] f. : hôtesse de l'air f. **72**
airport ['εəpɔːt] n. : aéroport n. m. **72**
aisle [aisl] n. : allée n. f. **80**
alarm clock [ə'lɑːmklɔk] : réveil n. m. **12, 31**; réveille-matin n. m. inv. **11**
a lot (of) [ə'lɔt(ɔv)] : beaucoup (de) **41, 56, 86**
always ['ɔːlwəz, -wiz] adv. : toujours **29**
amazing [ə'meiziŋ] adj. : étonnant, ante **69**
ambulance ['æmbjuləns] n. : ambulance n. f. **49**
anchor ['æŋkə'] n. : ancre n. f. **65**
angry ['æŋgri] adj. : en colère **57**
animal ['ænim(ə)l] n. : animal n. m. **68, 69, 76**
ankle boot ['æŋl(ə)lbuːt] : bottine n. f. **42**
anorak ['ænəræk] n. : anorak n. m. **87**
ant [ænt] n. : fourmi n. f. **91**
appearance [ə'piərəns] n. : aspect physique m. **36**
appearances [ə'piərənsiz] n. pl. : apparences n. f. pl. **27**
apple ['æpl] n. : pomme n. f. **53**
arithmetic [ə'riθmətik] n. : calcul n. m. **28**
arm [ɑːm] n. : bras n. m. **35, 47**
armchair ['ɑːmtʃεə'] n. : fauteuil n. m. **11**
arrival [ə'raiv(ə)l] n. : arrivée n. f. **72**
artist ['ɑːtist] n. : artiste **77**
ask for directions [ɑːskfɔː'd(a)i'rekʃ(ə)ns] : demander son chemin **18**
fall* asleep [fɔːlə'sliːp] v. : s'endormir* **62**
athlete ['æθliːt] n. : athlète **84**
at last [æt'lɑːst] adv. : enfin **30, 62**
audience ['ɔːdjəns] n. : public n. m. **78**
aunt [ɑːnt] n. f. : tante **34**
autumn ['ɔːtəm] n. : automne n. m. **60**

B

baby ['beibi] n. : bébé n. m. **35, 48**
babysitter ['beibisitə'] n. : baby-sitter n. f. **37**
back [bæk] n. : dos n. m. **46**; cour n. f. **93**
baker ['beikə'] n. : boulanger, ère **20**
bakery ['beikəri] n. : boulangerie n. f. **20**
balcony ['bælkəni] n. : balcon n. m. **9**
ball [bɔːl] n. : balle n. f. **86**; ballon n. m. **85, 75**; boule n. f. **90**
banana [bə'nɑːnə] n. : banane n. f. **53**
bank [bæŋk] n. : rive n. f. **64**
bank note ['bæŋknout] : billet n. m. **21**
bannisters ['bænistəz] n. pl. : rampe n. f. **10**
barometer [bə'rɔmitə'] n. : baromètre n. m. **67**
basket ['bɑːskit] n. : panier n. m. **91**
bat [bæt] n. : raquette n. f. **86**
bath [bɑːθ] n. : baignoire n. f. **15**
have* a bath [[hævə'bɑːθ] : prendre* un bain **15**

bathing suit [beiθiŋs(j)uːt] : maillot de bain m. **73**
bathrobe ['bɑːθroub] n. : peignoir n. m. **15**
bathroom ['bɑːθruːm] n. : salle de bains f. **15**
be* [biː] v. : être* **21, 35, 85**
beach [biːtʃ] n. : plage n. f. **73**
beach umbrella [biːtʃʌm'brelə] : parasol n. m. **73**
bead [biːd] n. : perle n. f. **43**
bear ['bεə'] n. : ours n. m. **30, 38**
beard [biəd] n. : barbe n. f. **37**
beautiful ['bjuːtif(u)l] adj. : beau, bel, belle **62, 93**
bed [bed] n. : lit n. m. **13**
bedroom ['bedru(:)m] n. : chambre n. f. **12**
bedside table ['bedsaidteibl] : table de chevet f. **11**
bee [biː] n. : abeille n. f. **63**
be* hungry [bi:'hʌŋgri] : avoir* faim **54**
be* late [bi:leit] : être* en retard **22**
believe [bi'liːv] v. : croire* **9**
belt [belt] n. : ceinture n. f. **41**
bench [ben(t)ʃ] n. : banc n. m. **81**
be* out of work [bi:autɔv'wɜːk] : être* au chômage **36**
best [best] adj. : meilleur, eure **29**
bet* [bet] v. : parier **52**
be* thirsty [bi:'θɜːsti] : avoir* soif **54, 81**
better ['betə'] adv. : mieux **72**
bicycle ['baisikl] n. : vélo n. m. **18**
big [big] adj. : grand **42**, large **40**
bike [baik] n. : vélo n. m. **19**
bird [bɜːd] n. : oiseau n. m. **61, 62**
birthday ['bɜːθdei] n. : anniversaire n. m. **92**
birthday party ['bɜːθdei'pɑːti] : goûter d'anniversaire m. **92**
black [blæk] adj. : noir, noire **29**
blackboard ['blækbɔːd] n. : tableau n. m. **26**
blanket ['blæŋkit] n. : couverture n. f. **11**
blond, blonde [blɔnd] adj. : blond, onde **37**
blouse [blauz] n. : chemisier n. m. **39**
blow* [blou] v. : souffler **65, 92**
blue [bluː] adj. : bleu, bleue **29**
boat [bout] n. : bateau n. m. **65**
body ['bɔdi] n. : corps n. m. **46, 47**
bone [boun] n. : os n. m. **54**
book [buk] n. : livre n. m. **11, 27, 30**
boot [buːt] n. : botte n. f. **42**
bottle [bɔtl] n. : bouteille n. f. **56**
bottom ['bɔtəm] n. : fesses n. f. pl. **46**
bouquet [bu'kei] n. : bouquet n. m. **63**
bow tie [boutai] : nœud papillon m. **39**
boy [bɔi] n. m. : garçon **35**
bracelet ['breislit] n. : bracelet n. m. **43**
branch [brɑːn(t)ʃ] n. : branche n. f. **60**
bread [bred] n. : pain n. m. **55**
break* [breik] v. : casser **14**
breakfast ['brekfəst] n. : petit déjeuner m. **55**
breast [brest] n. : aile n. f. **90**
breathe [briːθ] v. : respirer **49**
bridge [bridʒ] n. : pont n. m. **64**
brooch [broutʃ] n. : broche n. f. **43**
brook [bruk] n. : ruisseau n. m. **62**
brown [braun] adj. : marron adj. inv. **29**
brush one's teeth [brʌʃwʌnsti:θ] : se brosser les dents **15**

build* [bild] v. : construire* **64**
building ['bildiŋ] n. : immeuble n. m. **18**
building block ['bildiŋblɔk] : cube n. m. **75**
bullfighter [bulfaitə'] n. : torero n. m. **40**
bus [bʌs] n. : autobus n. m. **23**
bus fare [bʌsfεər] : ticket de bus m. **28**
bus stop [bʌsstɔp] : arrêt de bus m. **23**
butcher ['bʌtʃə'] n. : boucher n. m. **20**
butcher's shop ['bʌtʃəsʃɔp] : boucherie n. f. **20**
butter ['bʌtə'] n. : beurre n. m. **55**
butterfly ['bʌtəflai] n. : papillon n. m. **85**
butterfly net ['bʌtəflainet] : filet à papillons m. **85**
buy* [bai] v. : acheter **9, 21, 52**
bye ! [bai] interj. : au revoir ! **8, 14**

C

cabbage ['kæbidʒ] n. : chou n. m. **52**
cage [keidʒ] n. : cage n. f. **93**
cake [keik] n. : gâteau n. m. **14, 92**
calf pl. calves [kɑːf, kɑːvz] n. : veau n. m. **62**
camel ['kæm(ə)l] n. : chameau n. m. **76**
camera ['kæm(ə)rə] n. : appareil photo m. **91**
camp [kæmp] v. : faire* du camping **74**
camping ['kæmpiŋ] n. : camping n. m. **74**
camping car ['kæmpiŋkɑː'] : camping-car n. m. **74**
can* [kæn] v. : pouvoir* **80**
candle ['kænd(ə)l] n. : bougie n. f. **92**
canoe [kə'nuː] n. : canoë n. m. **64**
canvas ['kænvəs] n. : toile n. f. **77**
cap [kæp] n. : bonnet n. m. **41**; casquette n. f. **40**
car [kɑː'] n. : voiture n. f. **18, 19**
caravan ['kærəvæn] n. : caravane n. f. **74**
carnation [kɑ:'neiʃ(ə)n] n. : œillet n. m. **63**
car park [kɑː'pɑːk] : parking n. m. **18**
carriage ['kæridʒ] n. : wagon n. m. **22**
carrot ['kærət] n. : carotte n. f. **52**
cashier [kæ'ʃiə'] n. : caissier, ière **21**
cash register [kæʃ'redʒistə'] n. : caisse n. f. **21**
cat [kæt] n. : chat, chatte **68**
catch* [kætʃ] v. : attraper **76**; pêcher **64**
cause [kɔːz] v. : provoquer **19**
century ['sentjuri] n. : siècle n. m. **93**
cereal ['siəriəl] n. : céréales n. f. pl. **55**
chair [tʃεə'] n. : chaise n. f. **54**
chalet ['ʃælei] n. : chalet n. m. **61**
chamois ['ʃæmwɑː] n. : chamois n. m. **61**
champion ['tʃæmpiən] n. : champion, onne **84**
change [tʃein(d)ʒ] n. : monnaie n. f. **21**
change [tʃein(d)ʒ] v. : changer **79**
cheap [tʃiːp] adj. : bon marché adj. inv. **21**
check [tʃek] v. : vérifier **20**
checkers ['tʃekəz] n. pl. : jeu de dames m. **75**
cheek [tʃiːk] n. : joue n. f. **48**
cheese [tʃiːz] n. : fromage n. m. **56**
cherry ['tʃeri] n. : cerise n. f. **53**
chess [tʃes] n. : jeu d'échecs m. **75**
chestnut ['tʃes(t)nʌt] n. : châtaigne n. f. **60**

chicken ['tʃikin] n. : poulet n. m. 20, 56, 91
chief [tʃi:f] n. : chef n. m. 38
child pl. children [tʃaild, 'tʃildrən] n. : enfant 27, 35
chimney ['tʃimni] n. : cheminée n. f. 9
chin [tʃin] n. : menton n. m. 48
chocolate ['tʃɔklət] n. : chocolat n. m. 92
choose* [tʃu:z] v. : choisir 69
Christmas ['krisməs] n. : Noël n. m. 90
cinema ['sinəmə] n. : cinéma n. m. 80
circle ['sə:k(ə)l] n. : cercle n. m. 30
circus ['sə:kəs] n. : cirque n. m. 93
clap [klæp] v. : applaudir 78
class [klɑs] n. : classe n. f. 26
classroom ['klɑːsruːm] n. : salle de classe f. 26
clean [kliːn] adj. : propre 15
clean up [kliːnʌp] v. : faire* le ménage 34
clearing [kliəriŋ] n. : clairière n. f. 60
clock [klɔk] n. : horloge n. f. 22
close* [klouz] v. : fermer 84
closed [klouzd] adj. : fermé, ée 9, 20, 30
clothes [klouðz] n. pl. : vêtements n. m. pl. 39, 40, 41
cloud [klaud] n. : nuage n. m. 66
clown [klaun] n. : clown n. m. 93
coat [kout] n. : manteau n. m. 40
coatstand [kout'stænd] n. : portemanteau n. m. 40
cock [kɔk] n. : coq n. m. 68
coffee ['kɔfi] n. : café n. m. 55
coffee-pot ['kɔfipɔt] n. : cafetière n. f. 55
coin [kɔin] n. : pièce n. f. 21
cold [kould] adj. : froid, froide 74, 87, 91
colour ['kʌlər] n. : couleur n. f. 29
comb [koum] n. : peigne n. m. 15
come* back [kʌmbæk] v. : revenir* 64
comfortable ['kʌmfətəbl] adj. : confortable 11
competition [kɔmpi'tiʃ(ə)n] n. : concours n. m. 79
concentrate [kɔnsəntreit] v. : se concentrer 84
concert ['kɔnsət] n. : concert n. m. 78, 79
conductor [kən'dʌktər] n. : chef d'orchestre m. 78
cook [kuk] v. : faire* la cuisine 14
cooker ['kukər] n. : cuisinière n. f. 14
counter ['kauntər] n. : comptoir n. m. 21
country(side) ['kʌntri(said)] n. : campagne n. f. 62
court shoe [kɔːtʃuː] : escarpin n. m. 42
cousin ['kʌz(ə)n] n. : cousin, ine 34, 36
cow [kau] n. : vache n. f. 62
cream [kriːm] n. : crème n. f. 14
crocodile ['krɔkədail] n. : crocodile n. m. 69
cross (the street) [krɔs(θəstriːt)] v. : traverser (la rue) 18, 19
crossroads ['krɔsrouds] n. pl. : carrefour n. m. 18
cuckoo clock ['kukuːklɔk] : coucou n. m. 31
cup [kʌp] n. : tasse n. f. 55
cupboard ['kʌbəd] n. : placard n. m. 14
customs ['kʌstəms] n. pl. : douane n. f. 72
customs officer ['kʌstəms'ɔfisər] : douanier, ière 72
cut* [kʌt] v. : couper 35
cute [kjuːt] adj. : mignon, onne 48

D

daisy ['deizi] n. : marguerite n. f. 63
dance [dɑːns] n. : bal n. m. 39
dance [dɑːns] v. : danser 79
dangerous ['dein(d)ʒ(ə)rəs] adj. : dangereux, euse 62, 85
dark [dɑːk] adj. : sombre 10; foncé, ée 29; brun, une 37
daughter ['dɔːtər] n. f. : fille 34
day [dei] n. : jour n. m. 68
decide [di'said] v. : décider 68
deep [diːp] adj. : profond, onde 64
deer [diər] n. inv. : chevreuil n. m. 61
delicious [di'liʃəs] adj. : délicieux, ieuse 56, 60

departure [di'pɑːtjər] n. : départ n. m. 72
desk [desk] n. : bureau n. m. 26
die* [dai] v. : mourir* 49
dinner ['dinər] n. : dîner n. m. 57
diploma [di'ploumə] n. : diplôme n. m. 47
direction [d(a)i'rekʃ(ə)n] n. : direction n. f. 23
dirty ['də:ti] adj. : sale 15
dish [diʃ] n. : plat n. m. 54, 56
do* the dishes [du:θədiʃiz] : faire* la vaisselle 14
division [di'viʒ(ə)n] n. : division n. f. 28
doctor ['dɔktər] n. : médecin n. m. 49
dog [dɔg] n. : chien, chienne 68
doll [dɔl] n. : poupée n. f. 9, 75
dollar ['dɔlər] n. : dollar n. m. 28, 47
domino ['dɔminou] n. : domino n. m. 75
door [dɔːr] n. : porte n. f. 9
draught-board [drɑːftbɔːd] n. : damier n. m. 75
drawer ['drɔːər] n. : tiroir n. m. 41
drawing room ['drɔːiŋruːm] : salon n. m. 93
dress [dres] n. : robe n. f. 39
dressing gown ['dresiŋgaun] : robe de chambre f. 13
drink* [driŋk] v. : boire* 55
drive* [draiv] v. : conduire* 23, 62
drive* mad [draivmæd] : énerver 11
driver ['draivər] n. : conducteur, trice 23
drums [drʌms] n. pl. : batterie n. f. 79
duck [dʌk] n. : canard n. m. 68
dustbin ['dʌs(t)bin] n. : poubelle n. f. 14
dynamite ['dainəmait] n. : dynamite n. f. 19

E

eagle ['iːgl] n. : aigle n. m. 60, 61
ear ['iər] n. : oreille n. f. 48
early ['əːli] adv. : tôt 62
earring ['iːəriŋ] n. : boucle d'oreille f. 43
eat* [iːt] v. : manger 54, 56, 60, 77, 92
egg [eg] n. : œuf n. m. 55, 60, 61
eiderdown ['aidədaun] n. : édredon n. m. 13
elbow ['elbou] n. : coude n. m. 47
electric [i'lektrik] adj. : électrique 79
elephant ['elifənt] n. : éléphant n. m. 69
emerald ['em(ə)rəld] n. : émeraude n. f. 43
empty ['em(p)ti] adj. : vide 30
empty ['em(p)ti] v. : vider 57
end [end] n. : fin n. f. 93
engine ['endʒin] n. : locomotive n. f. 22
enthrall [in'θrɔːl] v. : captiver 80
excellent ['eksələnt] adj. : excellent, ente 26
exercise book ['eksəsaizbuk] : cahier n. m. 28
expensive [eks'pensiv] adj. : cher, ère 21, 77
explain [eks'plein] v. : expliquer 63
explanation [ekspla'neiʃ(ə)n] n. : explication n. f. 65
eye [ai] n. : œil n. m. 48, 84
eyebrow ['aibrau] n. : sourcil n. m. 48
eyelash ['ailæʃ] n. : cil n. m. 48

F

face [feis] n. : visage n. m. 48
faithful ['feiθf(u)l] adj. : fidèle 68
fall* [fɔːl] v. : tomber 60, 87
fall* asleep [fɔːlə'sliːp] v. : s'endormir* 62
family ['fæm(i)li] n. : famille n. f. 34
famous ['feiməs] adj. : célèbre 38
farm [fɑːm] n. : ferme n. f. 68
farmer ['fɑːmər] n. : fermier, ière 68
fat [fæt] adj. : gros, grosse 36
father ['fɑːðər] n. m. : père 34
fence [fens] n. : clôture n. f. 62
fertilizer ['fəːtilaizər] n. : engrais n. m. 52
fight* back [faitbæk] v. : se défendre* 80
figure ['figər] n. : chiffre n. m. 28
film [film] n. : film n. m. 80

find* [faind] v. : trouver 39, 60, 61
finger ['fiŋgər] n. : doigt n. m. 47
finish ['finiʃ] n. : arrivée n. f. 84
fire ['faiər] n. : feu n. m. 74
fireplace ['faiəpleis] n. : cheminée n. f. 90
first [fəːst] adj. : premier, ière 40, 93
first of all [fəːstəvɔːl] adv. : d'abord 92
fir tree [fəːtriː] : sapin n. m. 64
fish pl. fishes [fiʃ, 'fiʃiz] n. : poisson n. m. 57, 64, 76
fish bowl [fiʃboul] : aquarium n. m. 11
fisherman pl. -men ['fiʃəmæn, -men] n. m. : pêcheur, euse 64
fishing rod ['fiʃiŋrɔd] : canne à pêche f. 64
flat [flæt] n. : appartement n. m. 93
floor [flɔːr] n. : plancher n. m. 10; sol n. m. 43; étage n. m. 93
florist ['flɔrist] n. : fleuriste n. f. 63
flow [flou] v. : couler 64
flower ['flauər] n. : fleur n. f. 8, 63
flute [fluːt] n. : flûte n. f. 78
fly* [flai] v. : voler 62
flying saucer [flaiŋ'sɔːsər] : soucoupe volante f. 66
fog [fɔg] n. : brouillard n. m. 62
food [fuːd] n. : nourriture n. f. 51
foot pl. feet [fut, fiːt] n. : pied n. m. 42, 47
forbidden [fə'bidn] adj. : interdit, ite 18
forehead ['fɔːhed] n. : front n. m. 48
forest ['fɔrist] n. : forêt n. f. 60
forget* [fə'get] v. : oublier 22, 41, 84
fork [fɔːk] n. : fourchette n. f. 54
fountain ['fauntin] n. : fontaine n. f. 81
fridge [fridʒ] n. : réfrigérateur n. m. 57
friend [frend] n. : ami, ie 27
fringe [frindʒ] n. : frange n. f. 37
frown [fraun] v. : froncer les sourcils 46
fruit [fruːt] n. : fruits n. m. pl. 53
frying pan ['fraiŋpæn] : poêle n. f. 57
full [ful] adj. : plein, pleine 30
have* fun [hævfʌn] : s'amuser 27, 42, 75

G

game [geim] n. : jeu n. m. 75; partie n. f. 75; match n. m. 86
garage ['gærɑːʒ] n. : garage n. m. 9
garden ['gɑːd(ə)n] n. : jardin n. m. 8, 69
garland ['gɑːlənd] n. : guirlande n. f. 90
gentleman pl. -men ['dʒent(ə)lmæn, -men] n. m. : monsieur 23
get* changed [get'tʃein(d)ʒd] : se changer 92
get* dressed [get'dresd] v. : s'habiller 40
get* up [getʌp] v. : se lever 11
giraffe [dʒi'ræf, -'rɑːf] n. : girafe n. f. 69, 76
girl [gəːl] n. f. : fille 23, 35, 37, 39
give* [giv] v. : donner 92
glad [glæd] adj. : content, ente 74
glass [glɑːs] n. : verre n. m. 14, 54
glasses [glɑːsiz] n. pl. : lunettes n. f. pl. 46
glitter ['glitər] v. : briller 43
globe [gloub] n. : mappemonde n. f. 30
go* [gou] v. : aller* 20, 39, 57, 76
goat [gout] n. : chèvre n. f. 62
gold [gould] n. : or n. m. 43
goldfish ['gouldfiʃ] n. : poisson rouge m. 11
good [gud] adj. : bon, bonne 29, 79
go* to bed [goutu:bed] : aller* se coucher 75
grandfather ['græn(d)fɑːðər] n. m. : grand-père 34
grandmother ['græn(d)mʌðər] n. f. : grand-mère 34
grape [greip] n. : raisin n. m. 53
grass [grɑːs] n. : herbe n. f. 60
green [griːn] adj. : vert, verte 18, 29
green bean [griːnbiːn] : haricot vert m. 52
grey [grei] adj. : gris, grise 29
grill [gril] v. : faire* griller 74
grocer's shop ['grousəzʃɔp] : épicerie n. f. 20

on the ground [ɔnθəgraund] : par terre **27**
grow* [grou] v. : pousser **52**
guard [gɑ:d] v. : garder **68**
guest [gest] n. : invité, ée **40, 92**
guitar [gi'tɑ:ʳ] n. : guitare n. f. **74, 79**
gym [dʒim] n. : gymnase n. m. **85**
gymnastics [dʒim'næstiks] n. pl. :
  gymnastique n. f. **85**

H

hair ['hɛəʳ] n. : cheveux n. m. pl. **35, 48**;
  chevelure n. f. **37**
half an hour ['hɑ:fən'auəʳ] : demi-heure n. f. **35**
hall [hɔ:l] n. : couloir n. m. **10**
hand [hænd] n. : main n. f. **47**; aiguille n. f. **31**
hand basin [hænd'beis(ə)n] : lavabo n. m. **15**
hangar ['hæŋəʳ] n. : hangar n. m. **72**
hang* **up** ['hæŋʌp] v. : accrocher **67**
happen ['hæp(ə)n] v. : se passer **76**
happy ['hæpi] adj. : heureux, euse **35**; content,
  ente **30, 31, 38**; gai, gaie **15**
harbour ['hɑ:bəʳ] n. : port n. m. **65**
harp [hɑ:p] n. : harpe n. f. **79**
hat [hæt] n. : chapeau n. m. **40, 80**
head [hed] n. : tête n. f. **46**
have* **a bath** [[hævə'bɑ:θ] : prendre* un bain **15**
have* **a headache** [hævə'hedeik] : avoir* mal
  à la tête **49**
have* **fun** [hævfʌn] : s'amuser **27, 42, 75**
headlight ['hedlait] n. : phare n. m. **19**
headmaster [hed'mɑ:stəʳ] n. m. : directeur,
  trice **26**
health [helθ] n. : santé n. f. **49**
heart [hɑ:t] n. : cœur n. m. **49**
heavy ['hevi] adj. : lourd, lourde **22**
hectic ['hektik] adj. : agité, ée **66**
hedge [hedʒ] n. : haie n. f. **8**
heel [hi:l] n. : talon n. m. **42**
help [help] n. : aide n. f. **26**
help ! [help] interj. : au secours ! **72**
help [help] v. : aider **28, 87**
hen [hen] n. : poule n. f. **68**
henhouse ['henhaus] n. : poulailler n. m. **68**
hero ['hiərou] n. : héros n. m. **80**
hide* [haid] v. : se cacher **76**
hippopotamus pl. **-muses, -mi** [hipə'pɔtəməs,
  -məsiz, -mai] n. : hippopotame n. m. **69**
hold* [hould] v. : porter **35**
holiday ['hɔlidei] n. : fête n. f. **89**
holidays ['hɔlideiz] n. pl. : vacances n. f. pl. **22, 73**
homework ['houmwəːk] n. : devoirs n. m. pl. **28**
honey ['hʌni] n. : miel n. m. **55**
hoot [hu:t] v. : klaxonner **19**
hope [houp] v. : espérer **29**
horse [hɔ:s] n. : cheval n. m. **68**
hospital ['hɔspit(ə)l] n. : hôpital n. m. **49**
hour ['auəʳ] n. : heure n. f. **31, 35**
house [haus] n. : maison n. f. **7, 9, 10, 67, 68**
human ['hju:m(ə)n] adj. : humain, aine adj. **47**
be* **hungry** [bi:'hʌŋgri] : avoir* faim **54**
hunt [hʌnt] v. : chasser **38**
hurry ['hʌri] v. : se dépêcher **93**
husband ['hʌzbənd] n. m. : mari **34**

I

ice cream ['aiskri:m] : glace n. f. **92**
idea [ai'di:ə] n. : idée n. f. **66, 68**
impossible [im'pɔsibl] adj. : impossible **9**
Indian ['indiən] n. : Indien, ienne **64**
Indian ['indiən] adj. : indien, ienne **38**
influence ['influəns] n. : influence n. f. **26**
injection [in'dʒekʃ(ə)n] n. : piqûre n. f. **49**
inkwell ['iŋkwel] n. : encrier n. m. **30**
instrument ['instrumənt] n. : instrument n. m. **79**

invitation [invi'teiʃ(ə)n] n. : invitation n. f. **92**
invite [in'vait] v. : inviter **38**

J

jacket ['dʒækit] n. : veste n. f. **39, 40**
jam [dʒæm] n. : confiture n. f. **55**
jeans [dʒi:nz] n. pl. : jean n. m. **40**
jetty ['dʒeti] n. : jetée n. f. **65**
jewellery ['dʒu:əlri] n. : bijoux n. m. pl. **43**
job [dʒɔb] n. : travail n. m. **29**
juggler ['dʒʌgləʳ] n. : jongleur, euse **93**
juice [dʒu:s] n. : jus n. m. **92**
jump [dʒʌmp] v. : sauter **76, 84**

K

kangaroo [kæŋgə'ru:] n. : kangourou n. m. **76**
keep* **one's mouth shut** [ki:pwʌnsmauθʃʌt] :
  se taire* **38**
kennel ['ken(ə)l] n. : niche n. f. **68**
key [ki:] n. : clé n. f. **9**
kilo ['ki:lou] n. : kilo n. m. **20**
kitchen ['kitʃin] n. : cuisine n. f. **14, 57**
kite [kait] n. : cerf-volant n. m. **66, 91**
knee [ni:] n. : genou n. m. **47**
knife pl. **knives** [naif, naivz] n. : couteau n. m. **54**
know* [nou] v. : savoir* **29, 41, 60**

L

ladle ['leidl] n. : louche n. f. **57**
lady ['leidi] n. f. : dame n. f. **23, 46**
lamp [læmp] n. : lampe n. f. **11**
land [lænd] v. : atterrir **72**
landscape ['læn(d)skeip] n. : paysage n. m. **62**
late [leit] adv. : tard **13, 29**
be* **late** [bi:leit] : être* en retard **22**
lawn [lɔ:n] n. : pelouse n. f. **8**; gazon n. m. **8**
lawn mower ['lɔ:nmouəʳ] : tondeuse à gazon f. **8**
leaf pl. **leaves** [li:f, li:vz] n. : feuille n. f. **60**
learn* [lə:n] v. : apprendre* **27, 30**
leave* [li:v] v. : laisser **54**
leek [li:k] n. : poireau n. m. **52**
leg [leg] n. : jambe n. f. **47**; cuisse n. f. **56, 90**
leisure ['leʒəʳ] n. : loisirs n. m. pl. **71**
lemonade [lemə'neid] n. : limonade n. f. **92**
let* [let] v. : laisser **13**
lettuce ['letis] n. : salade n. f. **52**
light [lait] n. : lumière n. f. **10**
(traffic) light [('træfik)lait] n. : feu (de
  signalisation) n. m. **18**
light [lait] adj. : clair, claire **29**
lighthouse ['laithaus] n. : phare n. m. **65**
lightning ['laitniŋ] n. : éclair n. m. **67**
like [laik] v. : aimer **57**
lion ['laiən] n. : lion, lionne **69**
listen ['lis(ə)n] v. : écouter **30**
live [liv] v. : habiter **9**
lock [lɔk] n. : serrure n. f. **9**
log [lɔg] n. : bûche n. f. **90**
lollipop ['lɔlipɔp] n. : sucette n. f. **92**
long [lɔŋ] adj. : long, longue **37, 69**
look after [luk'ɑ:ftəʳ] v. : soigner **49**
look for [lukfɔ:ʳ] v. : chercher **93**
lorry ['lɔri] n. : camion n. m. **23**
love [lʌv] v. : aimer **8**
lovely ['lʌvli] adj. : beau, bel, belle **9, 31, 53**;
  joli, ie **39**
luck [lʌk] n. : chance n. f. **31**
luggage ['lʌgidʒ] n. : bagages n. m. pl. **22**
lunch [lʌn(t)ʃ] n. : déjeuner n. m. **56**
be* **lying down** [bi:laiŋdaun] : être* allongé,
  ée **47**

M

magic ['mædʒik] adj. : magique **52**
man pl. **men** [mæn, men] n. m. : homme **35**
marble ['mɑ:bl] n. : bille n. f. **27**
masseur, euse [mæ'səʳ, mæ'sə:z] n. : masseur,
  euse **47**
masterpiece ['mɑ:stəpi:s] n. : chef-d'œuvre
  n. m. **77**
mattress ['mætris] n. : matelas n. m. **11**
meadow ['medou] n. : prairie n. f. **62**
meal [mi:l] n. : repas n. m. **91**
meat [mi:t] n. : viande n. f. **56, 74**
medal ['med(ə)l] n. : médaille n. f. **84**
medicine ['med(i)sin] n. : médicament n. m.
  14, 49
mess [mes] n. : désordre n. m. **34**
microphone ['maikrəfoun] n. : micro n. m. **79**
milk [milk] n. : lait n. m. **21, 55**
minute ['minit] n. : minute n. f. **31**
mirror ['mirəʳ] n. : miroir n. m. **15**
make* **a mistake** [meikəmis'teik] : faire* une
  erreur **28**
mobile ['moubail] n. : mobile n. m. **75**
money ['mʌni] n. : argent n. m. **21**
monkey ['mʌŋki] n. : singe n. m. **69**
month [mʌnθ] n. : mois n. m. **93**
moon [mu:n] n. : lune n. f. **66**
morning ['mɔ:niŋ] n. : matin n. m. **52, 62**
moth [mɔθ] n. : mite n. f. **11**
mother ['mʌðəʳ] n. f. : mère **34**, maman **35**
motorcycle ['moutəsaikl] n. : moto n. f. **23**
mountain ['mauntin] n. : montagne n. f. **61**
mountain stream ['mauntinstri:m] : torrent
  n. m. **61**
moustache [məs'tɑ:ʃ] n. : moustache n. f. **37**
mouth [mauθ] n. : bouche n. f. **48**
multiplication [mʌltipli'keiʃ(ə)n] n. :
  multiplication n. f. **28**
muscled ['mʌsld] adj. : musclé, ée **47**
museum [mju(:)'ziəm] n. : musée n. m. **61**
mushroom ['mʌʃrum] n. : champignon n. m. **60**
music ['mju:zik] n. : musique n. f. **78, 79**
musician [mju'ziʃ(ə)n] n. : musicien, ienne **79**

N

napkin ['næpkin] n. : serviette n. f. **54**
narrow ['nærou] adj. : étroit, oite **10**
nature ['neitʃəʳ] n. : nature n. f. **59**
neck [nek] n. : cou n. m. **46, 69**
necklace ['neklis] n. : collier n. m. **43**
need [ni:d] v. : avoir* besoin **36**
nephew ['nefju] n. m. : neveu n. m. **55, 92**
nest [nest] n. : nid n. m. **60**
net [net] n. : filet n. m. **86**
new [nju:] adj. : nouveau, vel, velle **69**; neuf,
  neuve **39**
nice [nais] adj. : gentil, ille **38**
niece [ni:s] n. f. : nièce n. f. **37**
night [nait] n. : nuit n. f. **66**
nightcap ['naitkæp] n. : bonnet de nuit m. **13**
nose [nouz] n. : nez n. m. **48**
now [nau] adv. : maintenant **66, 72, 92**
nurse [nə:s] n. : infirmière n. f. **49**

O

okay ! ['ou'kei] interj. : d'accord ! **92**
old [ould] adj. : vieux, vieil, vieille **36**
omelet ['ɔmlit] n. : omelette n. f. **60**
onion ['ʌnjən] n. : oignon n. m. **52**
open ['oup(ə)n] adj. : ouvert, erte **30**
open ['oup(ə)n] v. : ouvrir* **84**
orange ['ɔrin(d)ʒ] n. : orange n. f. **53, 92**
orange ['ɔrin(d)ʒ] adj. : orange adj. inv. **29**

orchestra [ˈɔːkistrə] *n.* : orchestre *n. m.* **78**
ostrich [ɔˈstriʃ] *n.* : autruche *n. f.* **76**
other [ˈʌθəʳ] *adj.* : autre **76**
be* **out of work** [biːautɔvˈwəːk] : être* au chômage **36**
oven [ˈʌv(ə)n] *n.* : four *n. m.* **14**
owl [aul] *n.* : chouette *n. f.* **66**

P

page [peidʒ] *n.* : page *n. f.* **26**
paint [peint] *v.* : peindre* **77**
paint brush [peintˈbrʌʃ] : pinceau *n. m.* **77**
painting [ˈpeintiŋ] *n.* : peinture *n. f.* **77**; tableau *n. m.* **77, 93**
palette [ˈpælit] *n.* : palette *n. f.* **77**
palm tree [pɑːmtriː] : palmier *n. m.* **73**
paper [ˈpeipəʳ] *n.* : papier *n. m.* **77**
paper [ˈpeipəʳ] *v.* : tapisser **69**
parade [pəˈreid] *v.* : défiler **93**
parcel [ˈpɑːs(ə)l] *n.* : paquet *n. m.* **19**
park [pɑːk] *n.* : parc *n. m.* **81**
park [pɑːk] *v.* : stationner **18**
part [pɑːt] *n.* : partie *n. f.* : **47**
birthday **party** [ˈbəːθdeiˈpɑːti] : goûter d'anniversaire *m.* **92**
passenger [ˈpæsəndʒəʳ] *n.* : passager, ère **23**
passport [ˈpɑːspɔːt] *n.* : passeport *n. m.* **72**
path [pɑːθ] *n.* : allée *n. f.* **8**
pavement [ˈpeivmənt] *n.* : trottoir *n. m.* **18**
pay* [pei] *v.* : payer* **21**
pea [piː] *n.* : petit pois *m.* **52**
peach [piːtʃ] *n.* : pêche *n. f.* **53**
peak [piːk] *n.* : sommet *n. m.* **61**
pear [ˈpɛəʳ] *n.* : poire *n. f.* **53**
pebble [pebl] *n.* : caillou *n. m.* **64**
pedestrian [piˈdestriən] *n.* : piéton, onne **19**
peg [peg] *n.* : portemanteau *n. m.* **41**
pen [pen] *n.* : stylo *n. m.* **28**
pencil [ˈpens(ə)l] *n.* : crayon *n. m.* **77**
penguin [ˈpeŋgwin] *n.* : pingouin *n. m.* **76**
people [ˈpiːpl] *n.* : gens *n. m. pl.* **33**
pepper [ˈpepəʳ] *n.* : poivre *n. m.* **54**
performance [pəˈfɔːməns] *n.* : spectacle *n. m.* **93**
performer [pəˈfɔːməʳ] *n.* : artiste **93**
perhaps [pəˈhæps, præps] *adv.* : peut-être **49**
personality [pəːsəˈnæliti] *n.* : personnalité *n. f.* **38**
petal [pet(ə)l] *n.* : pétale *n. m.* **63**
petticoat [ˈpetikout] *n.* : jupon *n. m.* **39**
photo [ˈfoutou] *n.* : photo *n. f.* **46, 91**
take* a **photo** [teikəˈfoutou] : prendre* une photo **46, 91**
piano [piˈænou] *n.* : piano *n. m.* **78**
pick up [ˈpikʌp] *v.* : aller* chercher **37**
picnic [ˈpiknik] *n.* : pique-nique *n. m.* **91**
pig [pig] *n.* : cochon *n. m.* **62, 68**
pillow [pilou] *n.* : oreiller *n. m.* **13**
pineapple [ˈpainæpl] *n.* : ananas *n. m.* **53**
pink [piŋk] *adj.* : rose **29**
plait [plæt] *n.* : tresse *n. f.* **37**
plane [plein] *n.* : avion *n. m.* **72**
plant [plɑːnt] *n.* : plante *n. f.* **52, 63**
green **plant** [griːnˈplɑːnt] : plante verte *f.* **63**
plant [plɑːnt] *v.* : planter **8**
plate [pleit] *n.* : assiette *n. f.* **14, 54**
platform [ˈplætfɔːm] *n.* : quai *n. m.* **22**
play [plei] *v.* : jouer **27, 85, 86, 75, 78**
player [ˈpleiəʳ] *n.* : joueur, euse **86**
playground [ˈpleigraund] *n.* : cour *n. f.* **27**
playroom [ˈpleiruːm] *n.* : salle de jeux *f.* **75**
playtime [ˈpleitaim] *n.* : récréation *n. f.* **27**
pocket money [ˈpɔkitˈmʌni] : argent de poche *m.* **28**
podium *pl.* **-dia** [ˈpoudiəm, -diə] *n.* : podium *n. m.* **84**
police [pəˈliːs] *n.* : police *n. f.* **65**
policeman *pl.* **-men** [p(ə)ˈliːsmæn, -men] *n. m.* : agent de police *m.* **18**
polite [pəˈlait] *adj.* : poli, ie **38**

pond [pɔnd] *n.* : mare *n. f.* **68**
ponytail [ˈpouniteil] *n.* : queue de cheval *f.* **37**
poor [puəʳ] *adj.* : pauvre **38, 77**
portrait [ˈpɔːtreit] *n.* : portrait *n. m.* **77**
postman *pl.* **-men** [ˈpoustmæn, -men] *n. m.* : facteur *n. m.* **18**
post office [poustˈɔfis] : poste *n. f.* **18**
potato [p(ə)ˈteitou] *n.* : pomme de terre *f.* **52**
practical [ˈpræktik(ə)l] *adj.* : pratique **55**
present [ˈprezənt] *n.* : cadeau *n. m.* **90, 92**
price [prais] *n.* : prix *n. m.* **9**
projector [prəˈdʒektəʳ] *n.* : projecteur *n. m.* **80**
puddle [ˈpʌdl] *n.* : flaque *n. f.* **67**
pullover [ˈpulouvəʳ] *n.* : pull-over *n. m.* **41**
pumpkin [ˈpʌmpkin] *n.* : citrouille *n. f.* **52**
pupil [ˈpjuːp(i)l] *n.* : élève **26**
purple [ˈpəːpl] *adj.* : violet, ette **29**
purse [pəːs] *n.* : porte-monnaie *n. m. inv.* **21**
puschair [pʌstʃɛəʳ] *n.* : poussette *n. f.* **81**
put* [put] *v.* : poser **27**
puzzle [ˈpʌzl] *n.* : puzzle *n. m.* **75**
pyjamas [pəˈdʒɑːməs] *n. pl.* : pyjama *n. m.* **13**

Q

question [ˈkwestʃ(ə)n] *n.* : question *n. f.* **27**
quickly [ˈkwikli] *adv.* : vite **69**

R

rabbit [ˈræbit] *n.* : lapin *n. m.* **62**
race [reis] *n.* : course *n. f.* **84**
radish [ˈrædiʃ] *n.* : radis *n. m.* **52**
rain [rein] *n.* : pluie *n. f.* **52, 67**
rain [rein] *v.* : pleuvoir* **52**
raincoat [ˈreinkout] *n.* : imperméable *n. m.* **40, 67**
raise [reiz] *n.* : augmentation *n. f.* **28**
rake [reik] *n.* : râteau *n. m.* **8**
read* [riːd] *v.* : lire* **11**
real [ˈriəl] *adj.* : vrai, vraie **57, 64**
really [ˈriəli] *adv.* : vraiment **55, 77**
record [riˈkɔːd] *n.* : disque *n. m.* **37**
rectangle [ˈrektæŋgl] *n.* : rectangle *n. m.* **30**
red [red] *adj.* : rouge **29**
red-haired [ˈredˈhɛəd] *adj.* : roux, rousse **37**
rent [rent] *v.* : louer **9, 93**
rice [rais] *n.* : riz *n. m.* **56**
rich [ritʃ] *adj.* : riche **38**
ride* a horse [raidəˈhɔːs] : monter à cheval **68**
rider [ˈraidəʳ] *n.* : écuyer, ère **93**
ring [riŋ] *n.* : bague *n. f.* **43**; piste *n. f.* **93**
ring* [riŋ] *v.* : sonner **11, 31**
ripe [raip] *adj.* : mûr, mûre **53**
river [ˈrivəʳ] *n.* : rivière *n. f.* **64**
road sign [roudsain] : panneau (de signalisation) *n. m.* **23**
roll [roul] *v.* : rouler **43**
roller skate [ˈrouləʳskeit] : patin à roulettes *m.* **85**
roof [ruːf] *n.* : toit *n. m.* **9, 68**
rose [rouz] *n.* : rose *n. f.* **63**
round [raund] *adj.* : rond, ronde **30**
rubber [ˈrʌbəʳ] *n.* : gomme *n. f.* **77**
rubber ring [ˈrʌbəʳriŋ] : bouée *n. f.* **73**
ruby [ˈruːbi] *n.* : rubis *n. m.* **43**
rucksack [ˈrʌksæk] *n.* : sac à dos *m.* **74**
rug [rʌg] *n.* : tapis *n. m.* **11**
ruler [ˈruːləʳ] *n.* : règle *n. f.* **77**
run* [rʌn] *v.* : courir* **27, 69, 84**
runway [ˈrʌnwei] *n.* : piste *n. f.* **72**

S

sail [seil] *n.* : voile *n. f.* **65**
sale [seil] *n.* : soldes *n. m. pl.* **31**
salesperson [seilzˈpəːs(ə)n] : vendeur, euse **21**

salt [sɔlt] *n.* : sel *n. m.* **54**
sand castle [sændkɑːs(ə)l] : château de sable *m.* **73**
sand [sænd] *n.* : sable *n. m.* **73**
sandal [ˈsænd(ə)l] *n.* : sandale *n. f.* **47**
sandwich [ˈsændwitʃ] *n.* : sandwich *n. m.* **91**
satchel [ˈsætʃ(ə)l] *n.* : cartable *n. m.* **28**
saucepan [ˈsɔːspən] *n.* : casserole *n. f.* **14**
saxophone [ˈsæksəfoun] *n.* : saxophone *n. m.* **79**
say* [sei] *v.* : dire* **42**
school [skuːl] *n.* : école *n. f.* **25, 26, 27, 30**
schoolteacher [ˈskuːltiːtʃəʳ] *n.* : maître, maîtresse **26**
scream [skriːm] *v.* : crier **80**
screen [skriːn] *n.* : écran *n. m.* **80**
sea [siː] *n.* : mer *n. f.* **65**
seagull [ˈsiːgʌl] *n.* : mouette *n. f.* **66**
seat [siːt] *n.* : fauteuil *n. m.* **80**
second [ˈsekənd] *n.* : seconde *n. f.* **31**
second [ˈsekənd] *adj.* : deuxième **93**
see* [siː] *v.* : voir* **34, 46, 52, 53, 56, 67, 76, 80**
see you soon ! [siːjusuːn] *interj.* : à bientôt ! **8, 22**
sell* [sel] *v.* : vendre* **9, 21**
shampoo [ʃæmˈpuː] *n.* : shampooing *n. m.* **15**
shape [ʃeip] *n.* : forme *n. f.* **30**
sheet [ʃiːt] *n.* : drap *n. m.* **11**
shelf *pl.* **shelves** [ʃelf, ʃelvz] *n.* : étagère *n. f.* **14**
shell [ʃel] *n.* : coquillage *n. m.* **73**
shelter [ˈʃeltəʳ] *v.* : s'abriter **67**
shine* [ʃain] *v.* : briller **66, 73**
ship [ʃip] *n.* : navire *n. m.* **65**
shirt [ʃəːt] *n.* : chemise *n. f.* **41**
shoe [ʃuː] *n.* : chaussure *n. f.* **42, 67**
shoelace [ˈʃuːleis] *n.* : lacet *n. m.* **42**
shop [ʃɔp] *n.* : magasin *n. m.* **20**, boutique *n. f.* **20**
shop [ʃɔp] *v.* : faire* les courses **20**
short [ʃɔːt] *adj.* : court, courte **37, 40**
shorts [ʃɔːts] *n. pl.* : short *n. m.* **85**
shoulder [ˈʃouldəʳ] *n.* : épaule *n. f.* **46**
shovel [ˈʃʌv(ə)l] *n.* : pelle *n. f.* **8**
show* [ʃou] *v.* : montrer* **77**; indiquer **31**
show* the way [ʃouθəˈwei] : montrer le chemin **18**
shutter [ˈʃʌtəʳ] *n.* : volet *n. m.* **9**
sick [sik] *adj.* : malade **49**
singer [ˈsiŋəʳ] *n.* : chanteur, euse **79**
sing* out of tune [siŋautɔvtjuːn] : chanter faux **79**
sink [siŋk] *n.* : évier *n. m.* **14**
sink* [siŋk] *v.* : couler **64**
be* **sitting down** [biːsitiŋdaun] : être* assis, se **11**
sitting-room [ˈsitiŋru(ː)m] *n.* : salon *n. m.* **69**, salle de séjour *f.* **11**
skate board [ˈskeitbɔːd] : planche à roulettes *f.* **85**
ski [skiː] *n.* : ski *n. m.* **87**
ski [skiː] *v.* : skier **87**
ski hat [skihæt] : bonnet *n. m.* **87**
skiing [skiiŋ] *n.* : ski *n. m.* **87**
skirt [skəːt] *n.* : jupe *n. f.* **40**
sky [skai] *n.* : ciel *n. m.* **66**
sleep* [sliːp] *v.* : dormir* **13, 74**
sleeping bag [ˈsliːpiŋbæg] : sac de couchage *m.* **74**
sleepwalker [ˈsliːpwɔːkəʳ] *n.* : somnambule **57**
sleigh [slait] *n.* : luge *n. f.* **87**
slide [slaid] *n.* : toboggan *n. m.* **81**, barrette *n. f.* **37**
slide* [slaid] *v.* : glisser **81**
slipper [ˈslipəʳ] *n.* : chausson *n. m.* **41**
slope [sloup] *n.* : piste *n. f.* **87**
small [smɔːl] *adj.* : petit, ite **36**
smart [smɑːt] *adj.* : élégant, ante **39**
smile [smail] *v.* : sourire* **91**
smock [smɔk] *n.* : tablier *n. m.* **77**
smoke [smouk] *n.* : fumée *n. f.* **74**
snake [sneik] *n.* : serpent *n. m.* **69**
snow [snou] *n.* : neige *n. f.* **87**
snow [snou] *v.* : neiger **87**
snowball [ˈsnoubɔːl] *n.* : boule de neige *f.* **87**
snowman *pl.* **-men** [snoumæn, -men] *n. m.* : bonhomme de neige **87**

soap [soup] n. : savon n. m. 15
sock [sɔk] n. : chaussette n. f. 41
solution [sə'lu:ʃ(ə)n] n. : solution n. f. 55
son [sʌn] n. m. : fils 34
soon [su:n] adv. : bientôt 11
be * sorry [bi:'sɔri] : être * désolé, ée 38
soup [su:p] n. : soupe n. f. 57
soup tureen [su:ptjuə'ri:n] : soupière n. f. 57
spectator [spek'teitə'] n. : spectateur, trice 93
sponge [spʌn(d)ʒ] n. : éponge n. f. 14
spoon [spu:n] n. : cuillère n. f. 54
sportsgear [spɔ:tsgiə'] n. : équipement n. m. 85
sport [spɔ:t] n. : sport n. m. 83
spring ['spriŋ] n. : printemps n. m. 8
square ['skwɛə'] n. : carré n. m. 30
squirrel ['skwir(ə)l] n. : écureuil n. m. 60
orange squeezer ['ɔrin(d)ʒ'skwi:zə'] : presse-
    fruits n. m. inv. 36
stadium ['steidiəm] n. : stade n. m. 84
stag [stæg] n. : cerf n. m. 76
stage [steidʒ] n. : scène n. f. 78
stain [stein] n. : tache n. f. 77
stairs ['stəz] n. pl. : escalier n. m. 10
stamp [stæmp] n. : timbre n. m. 21
stand * [stænd] v. : supporter 42
be * standing up [bi:stændiŋʌp] : être * debout 47
star [sta:'] n. : étoile n. f. 66
starch [sta:tʃ] n. : amidon n. m. 87
starving ['sta:viŋ] adj. : affamé, ée 77
station ['steiʃ(ə)n] n. : gare n. f. 22
stem [stem] n. : tige n. f. 63
step [step] n. : marche n. f. 10
stereo ['steriou] n. : chaîne stéréo f. 11
stomach ['stʌmək] n. : ventre n. m. 46
stool [stu:l] n. : tabouret n. m. 14
storm [stɔ:m] n. : orage n. m. 67
straight [streit] adj. : raide 37
strange [strein(d)ʒ] adj. : bizarre 42
strawberry ['strɔ:b(ə)ri] n. : fraise n. f. 53
street [stri:t] n. : rue n. f. 18, 93
stripe [straip] n. : rayure n. f. 29
strong [strɔŋ] adj. : fort, forte 36, 85
stuff [stʌf] v. : farcir 20
stuffing ['stʌfiŋ] n. : farce n. f. 20
sturdy ['stə:di] adj. : solide 64
subtraction [səb'trækʃ(ə)n] n. : soustraction
    n. f. 28
sugar ['ʃugə'] n. : sucre n. m. 21, 55
sugar dispenser ['ʃugə'dis'pensə'] : sucrier
    n. m. 55
suit [s(j)u:t] n. : costume n. m. 39, 41
suitcase ['s(j)u:tkeis] n. : valise n. f. 22
summer ['sʌmə'] n. : été n. m. 73
sun [sʌn] n. : soleil n. m. 62, 73
sunglasses ['sʌngla:siz] n. pl. : lunettes de
    soleil f. pl. 73
sun-tanned ['sʌntænd] adj. : bronzé, ée 73
supermarket [s(j)u:'pəma:kit] n. :
    supermarché n. m. 20
sure ['ʃuə'] adj. : sûr, sûre 20
surprise [sə'praiz] n. : surprise n. f. 14, 38
sweet [swi:t] n. : bonbon n. m. 28, 92
sweet pepper [swi:t'pepə'] : poivron n. m. 52
swim * [swim] v. : nager * 65, 68
swing [swiŋ] n. : balançoire n. f. 81
synthesizer ['sinθəsaizə'] n. : synthétiseur
    n. m. 79
syringe ['sirindʒ, si'rindʒ] n. : seringue n. f. 49

T

table ['teibl] n. : table n. f. 54
tablecloth ['teiblklɔθ] n. : nappe n. f. 56
table tennis ['teibl'tenis] : tennis de table m. 86
take * a photo [teikə'foutou] : prendre * une
    photo 46, 91
take * off ['teikɔf] v. : décoller 72

talk * [tɔ:k] v. : parler 76
tall [tɔ:l] adj. : grand, grande 36
tamer ['teimə'] n. : dompteur, euse 93
tap [tæp] n. : robinet n. m. 15
tart [ta:t] n. : tarte n. f. 56
taxi ['tæksi] n. : taxi n. m. 23
tea [ti:] n. : thé n. m. 55
teacher ['ti:tʃə'] n. : professeur n. m. 27
teapot ['ti:pɔt] n. : théière n. f. 55
teddy bear ['tedibɛə'] : ours en peluche m. 75
tee-shirt ['ti:ʃə:t] n. : tee-shirt n. m. 41
telephone ['telifoun] n. : téléphone n. m. 11
make * a telephone call [meikə'telifounkɔ:l] :
    téléphoner 19
telephone kiosk ['telifounkiɔ:sk] : cabine
    téléphonique f. 19
television [teli'viʒ(ə)n] n. : télévision n. f. 11
tell * [tel] v. : dire * 52
tennis shoe ['tenisʃu:] : tennis n. m. 42
tent [tent] n. : tente n. f. 74
thanks ! [θæŋks] interj. : merci ! 28, 36
thin [θin] adj. : maigre 36
think * [θiŋk] v. : penser 87; croire * 35, 43
be * thirsty [bi:'θə:sti] : avoir * soif 54, 81
throw * [θrou] v. : lancer * 87
thunder ['θʌndə'] n. : tonnerre n. m. 67
ticket collector ['tikitkə'lektə'] : contrôleur
    n. m. 22
tie [tai] n. : cravate n. f. 39
tights [taits] n. pl. : collant n. m. 39
time [taim] n. : heure n. f. 14, 31
tired ['taid] adj. : fatigué, ée 13
today [tə'dei] adv. : aujourd'hui 27, 60, 72
toe [tou] n. : doigt de pied m. 47
tomato [tə'ma:tou] n. : tomate n. f. 91
tomorrow [tə'mɔrou] adv. : demain 31, 52
tongue [tʌŋ] n. : langue n. f. 48
tonight [tə'nait] adv. : ce soir 39
too [tu:] adv. : trop 40, 42, 62, 85; aussi 75
tooth pl. teeth [tu:θ, ti:θ] n. : dent n. f. 15, 48
toothbrush ['tu:θbrʌʃ] n. : brosse à dents f. 15
toothpaste ['tu:θpeist] n. : dentifrice n. m. 15
total ['tout(ə)l] n. : total n. m. 28
towel ['tauəl] n. : serviette n. f. 15
town [taun] n. : ville n. f. 17, 29
toy [tɔi] n. : jouet n. m. 75
track [træk] n. : voie n. f. 22; trace n. f. 30;
    piste n. f. 84; chemin n. m. 61
tracksuit ['træks(j)u:t] n. : jogging n. m. 85
traffic ['træfik] n. : circulation n. f. 19
traffic jam ['træfikdʒæm] : embouteillage
    n. m. 18, 19
train [trein] n. : train n. m. 22
transport ['træns:pɔ:t] n. : moyens de
    transport m. pl. 23
tree [tri:] n. : arbre n. m. 8, 60, 90
triangle ['traiæŋgl] n. : triangle n. m. 30
trousers ['trauzəz] n. pl. : pantalon n. m. 40
trumpet ['trʌmpit] n. : trompette n. f. 78
trunk [trʌŋk] n. : tronc n. m. 60
try * [trai] v. : essayer * 65
tube of paint [tju:bɔvpeint] : tube de peinture
    m. 77
tulip ['tju:lip] n. : tulipe n. f. 63
turkey ['tə:ki] n. : dinde n. f. 90
tyre ['taiə'] n. : pneu n. m. 19

U

ugly ['ʌgli] adj. : laid, laide 36
umbrella [ʌm'brelə] n. : parapluie n. m. 67
umpire ['ʌmpaiə'] n. : arbitre n. m. 86
uncle ['ʌŋkl] n. : oncle n. m. 14, 34
understand * [ʌndə'stænd] v. : comprendre * 30

V

valley ['væli] n. : vallée n. f. 61
vase [va:z] n. : vase n. m. 11
vegetables ['vedʒ(i)təbls] n. pl. : légumes
    n. m. pl. 52
very ['veri] adv. : très 39, 62
vest [vest] n. : maillot n. m. 85
viewer ['vju:ə'] n. : spectateur, trice 80
violin [vaiə'lin] n. : violon n. m. 78

W

wait (for) [weit(fɔ:')] v. : attendre * 23, 60, 62,
    69, 92
wake * up ['weikʌp] v. : se réveiller 11
walkie-talkie [wɔ:ki'tɔki] n. : talkie-walkie
    n. m. 61
wall [wɔ:l] n. : mur n. m. 9
wallet ['wɔlit] n. : portefeuille n. m. 21
wallpaper ['wɔ:lpeipə'] n. : papier peint m. 69
want [wɔnt] v. : vouloir * 20, 29, 53
wardrobe ['wɔ:droub] n. : armoire n. f. 11;
    penderie n. f. 41
warm oneself [wɔ:mwʌn'self] v. : se
    réchauffer 74
wash oneself [wɔʃwʌn'self] v. : se laver 15
watch [wɔtʃ] n. : montre n. f. 31, 48
watch (over) [wɔtʃ('ouvə')] v. : surveiller 27
watch television [wɔtʃteli'viʒ(ə)n] : regarder la
    télévision 11
water ['wɔ:tə'] n. : eau n. f. 57
water ['wɔ:tə'] v. : arroser 8
watering can ['wɔ:təriŋkæn] : arrosoir n. m. 8
water-ski * ['wɔ:tə'ski:] v. : faire * du ski
    nautique 65
wear * [wɛə'] v. : porter 39, 46
weather ['weðə'] n. : temps n. m. 67
weathercock ['weðəkɔk] n. : girouette n. f. 68
week [wi:k] n. : semaine n. f. 28
weigh [wei] v. : peser 20
weights [weits] n. pl. : haltères n. m. pl. 85
well [wel] adv. : bien 34, 77, 86
wet [wet] adj. : mouillé, ée 67
white [(h)wait] adj. : blanc, blanche 29
wife pl. wives [waif, waivz] n. f. : femme 34
wild [waild] adj. : sauvage 69
wilted ['wiltid] adj. : fané, ée 63
win * [win] v. : gagner 86, 84
wind [wind] n. : vent n. m. 65
window ['windou] n. : fenêtre n. f. 9
winner ['winə'] n. : vainqueur n. m. 84
winter ['wintə'] n. : hiver n. m. 87
woman pl. -men ['wumən, -min] n. f. : femme
    35, 72, dame 22
wood [wud] n. : bois n. m. 74
work [wə:k] n. : travail n. m. 52
work hard [wə:kha:d] : bien travailler 26
worried ['wʌrid] adj. : inquiet, ète 49
write * [rait] v. : écrire * 26

Y

yawn [jɔ:n] v. : bâiller 13
yellow ['jelou] adj. : jaune 29
yogurt ['jɔgət] n. : yaourt n. m. 56
young [jʌŋ] adj. : jeune 35

Z

zebra ['zi:brə, 'zebrə] n. : zèbre n. m. 69, 76
zebra crossing ['zi:brəkrɔsiŋ] : passage pour
    piétons m. 23
zoo [zu:] n. : zoo n. m. 76

Printed in Spain
by Graficromo, S.A. Córdoba